KANYA

KANYA
Exploitation of Little Angels

Dr. (Mrs.) V. Mohini Giri

GYAN

GYAN PUBLISHING HOUSE

NEW DELHI-110002

KANYA : Emancipation of Little Angels
(*Sociology, Women's Studies*)

ISBN: 81- 212-0623-5

Published in 1999 by
Gyan Publishing House,
5, Ansari Road, Darya Ganj
New Delhi-110002

Laser Typesetting at Elite Art, New Delhi-2
Printed at Mehra Offset Press, Delhi

Children live what they learn.
If a child lives with criticism, he learns to condemn.
If a child lives with hostility, he learns to fight.
If a child lives with ridicule, he learns to be shy.
If a child lives with shame, he learns to feel guilty.
If a child lives with tolerance, he learns to be patient.
If a child lives with encouragement, he learns confidence.
If a child lives with praise, he learns to appreciate.
If a child lives with fairness, he learns justice.
If a child lives with security, he learns to have faith.
If a child lives with approval, he learns to like himself.
If a child lives with acceptance and friendship,
he learns to find love in the world.

DOROTHY LAW HOLTZ

Contents

Message

If development of women and children, constituting more than fifty per cent of the country's population, is to be the prime determinant of the level of civilisation, then despite universal pledges, covenants and declarations, this message is yet to be taken seriously by the world community. Women and children in the country continue to face deprivation, poverty, physical and emotional abuse and worst of all, sexual abuse.

The nature, extent and the intricacies of the problem of trafficking and prostitution of women and children is difficult to gauge because the business requires to be shrouded in ambiguity. Dr. (Mrs.) V. Mohini Giri, as Chairperson of the National Commission for Women, after visiting hundreds of places in the country and having acquired first hand knowledge about the extent of the problem, has in this book, vividly explained in great detail the phenomena.

One fact that forcefully emerges is that women and girls in prostitution belong to the most disadvantaged section of society. I congratulate Mrs. Mohini Giri on her accomplishment. Her crusade against injustice and for heralding an era of gender justice is commendable as will be seen from this work. Let these efforts bear fruit. I have no doubt that this publication will help in sensitizing the concerned to give a fair deal to women and children.

Baba Amte

Foreword

I am happy to have been asked to write the foreword for Shrimati Mohini Giri's book titled "Kanya". In October 1993, I joined the National Human Rights Commission as its first Chairman. By then the National Commission for Women had been constituted. Under the Protection of Human Rights Act, the Commission has five members and three deemed members—one of the deemed members being the Chairperson of the National Commission for Women. I had known Shrimati Giri earlier but was not acquainted with her manner of functioning. At the first meeting of the Commission I noticed her spirited approach, determination to act and achieve results. I also marked her concern for the Indian woman. She had very clear views about the problems faced in our society but she had answers to these problems and the methodology for solution too. She was not happy with her powers under the statute which set-up the National Commission for Women. The absence of an effective investigation agency bothered her the most. We agreed to allow the investigation agency of the Human Rights Commission to be available to her in suitable cases and she agreed to refer or transfer such of the cases which in her opinion called for immediate in-depth investigation. After all, violation of human rights of women also gave rise to a situation for invoking our jurisdiction. In an enlarged sense, we could be treated as one Commission.

We soon came to realize that considering the prevailing situation, steps for protection of women's rights deserved priority of action and perhaps concentrated attention. If I remember correctly, at her instance we investigated some cases of rape, of making women walk nude in the public in rural areas and ill-treatment at police stations.

The overall situation in the country made her restless. She moved across the entire country to respond to every woman in distress. One of the areas which bothered her most is prostitution—a social malady as old as the formation of human society. The gender bias, ill-treatment of the girl-child, particularly by her own parents within the family and child prostitution which has emerged enormously as a recent feature of the sex trade led her to attack the institution of prostitution in general and child prostitution in particular.

The appearance of AIDS and induction of children into the sex trade disturbed her very much. The two Commissions formulated a coordinated course of action for meeting the situation in Delhi. She spread the drive in Mumbai and Calcutta also. Gradually, she spread her message all over the country. In a short period, she has succeeded in bringing this burning issue to the fore; but the problem is as obstinate as ever.

Shrimati Giri is a dauntless fighter. She has realized that fighting in the field has to be coordinated with the spread of the message to reach every heart. That has led her to write this book.

I must say that this book is different from many other books on the topic. It has the full support of experience and is perhaps an account of the action of a soldier who has fairly succeeded in the fight. The war is such that it has no end. No one can fully succeed until everyone in the society joins the struggle and binds himself or herself by an oath to keep out of the trade and help others to do so.

This is not a trade of men only. At many places women run the show. In some cases parents too lead their minor girls into the trade. It may be difficult to totally stop the profession but certainly we can keep the minor and the incapable of deciding upon her course of life, out of the flesh trade and leave the elder ones to make their own choice after being aware of the attendant killer diseases.

I am sure the reader will find Mrs. Girl's book engrossing and an eye opener. She has succeeded in arousing the sympathy of everyone for the 'thorn buds' and would be happy if her book achieves the securing of the reader's support for the cause so dear to her heart. My earnest and whole-hearted wishes for the endeavour.

New Delhi
27th July, 1998

Ranganath Misra
Justice (Retd.)

Preface

The century is agog with the Bomb! Post-Bomb Budget and the Soccer World Cup—watching the television and ads in between—I wonder if we have really progressed! Does everyone have enough to eat? Is there no poverty and no economic deprivation?

What is the reason for little children, both physically and mentally defenceless, being pushed into the flesh trade? At the National Commission for Women, for the past three years, I have been seeking answers and solutions to these vexing problems. It is a difficult path but I firmly believe that I shall surmount all obstacles and reach the goal. My dream to see the Indian girl-child—as a child and not a girl-woman burdened with troubles on her shoulders that must materialise. Abuse of children is the most heinous crime and exploiters of girls should be given exemplary punishment.

In these pages I have poured out my anguish for this problem. In this task many people have given me hope, direction, guidance, help and sympathy. A big loving 'Thank You' is conveyed to Dipti Bhargava, Bhamati Nair, Shyamala Natarajan, Meena Seshu, Indrani Sinha, Dr. Mukherjee, Roma Debabrata, Jyotsna Chatterjee, Asha Ramesh, Vijji Srinivasan, Celsa Antao, Champa Ben, Shri Ram Snehi, Dr. Patil, Ms. Roda Mistry and Ms. Indira Ben.

I am deeply indebted to Justice Ranganath Misra, M.P. for writing the Foreword to this book.

It was very gracious of Baba Amte that he listened to me patiently about this work. His blessings and the message have given me immense encouragement. I am extremely thankful to him for his kindness and generosity.

My respectful gratitude is acknowledged to my guru Justice Krishna Iyer and brother Justice V.S. Malimath.

My blessings are reserved to B.V.N. Lakshmi without whose support and valuable time the anguished episodes could not have been recounted and a fond thank you to Dr. P.S.K. Menon.

I hope that this book will not be put aside as just another publication and will receive its due place. If the account rendered here is able to arouse the conscience of the readers and sensitise them on the issue, I would consider my efforts amply rewarded.

New Delhi **V. Mohini Giri**
Independence Day

1

Face to Face

Who is the purchaser of the girl's virginity? Who is the highest bidder to have the right to spend the first night with a small girl? Who is it who wants the company of women while travelling, or while staying alone in a city? Who are those people who come with false promises of marriages and jobs? Who are the people who sell their little daughters for economic reasons? Aren't they all really our uncles, our brothers, our fathers...all of them men?

Commercial sexual exploitation of children is an all pervasive abnoxious global problem. At present it is one of the major flourishing trades. No civilised society should tolerate this form of violence on innocent young vulnerable children which is a potential national human resource. Today, it is a universally recognised fact that child abuse constitutes a gross violation of the child's right to protection and healthy development. It is also a flourishing industry operating worldwide that capitalizes on the sale and trafficking of children through Internet and other means. Hence it is of serious concern to multidisciplinarians. This is a multifaceted problem which needs well planned multipronged strategies for its eradication. However, all these global and national efforts need a micro-level understanding of the situation in different regions if they are to succeed.

India, with 28,000 kms of spanning dimension and a rich tradition of civilisation, inhabited by people of diverse economic levels and cultural attainments, speaking a variety of languages, is a country which presents a distinct flavour of the high and the low, the ugly and the beautiful. These contradictions are nowhere more manifest as in the case of prostitution and child prostitution owing to the steady increase in the levels of income, different levels of affluence as a result of international trade, economic liberalisation and the green and white revolutions. The scene is indeed pathetic when we discuss child prostitution!

We find ourselves today at a particular historical juncture, where progress and development in human society has created two contradictions. On the one hand, there is modernity with improved quality of life while on the other, the same change threatens many aspects of community life, such as the loss of ethics and moral values to the corrupting influence of modernity itself.

We have a growing population of children and young people exposed not only to the seduction of capitalism, but also to the economic pressures for survival. The social conditions emerging out of this phenomenon become fertile ground for the easy recruitment of innocent victims into the vicious market of human flesh.

In many areas of our country women are forced into prostitution or flesh trade in the name of religion and culture. The induction of adolescent girls into the sex trade takes place with the full knowledge and even the connivance of family members. The practice of this 'contemporary form of slavery' needs to be brought to the foreground of development concerns, and eliminated. This is an intolerable form of child labour and abuse of the child. In India sexual exploitation of children has its roots in traditional practices, beliefs and gender discrimination. The problem of child prostitution in India is more complicated than in other Third World countries where it is directly related to sex tourism.

Like child labour, child prostitution is almost everywhere. It runs the sordid gamut from incest and sexual abuse by friends and family members to the systematic commercial plundering of children and young teenagers in lucrative prostitution and pornography markets.

The very basis of the child sex industry—designation of a child as a commodity for sale and purchase—demeans and dehumanizes the child. It also serves the sexual drive of sexually immature men who seek emotional release by exploiting a completely powerless slave child.

On a sticky morning as I opened the newspaper, to my surprise I read the headline screaming "Five hundred little children from Kamathipura raided and taken into custody". Having read the headline I stood up and wondered what would be happening to the children? Something had to be done urgently. Upon receiving information that these children were in police custody, Ms. Padma Seth and myself rushed to the police station and were met with the tearful faces of 500 little girls who had no food to eat, no toilets to ease themselves and no place to sit. They were huddled like sheep together with tears rushing down their eyes.

Any rescue work that has to be carried on must be with prior arrangements made and thought given to where such people would be accommodated. The Maharashtra Government could not find homes for these girls for nearly 48 hours and even after they found those homes, they were not the places where little girls could get security! Many of the girls who were huddled like sheep told us that they left behind at the brothel their infants and precious hard earned belongings while some girls were having periods with no support services. Each girl clamoured to be sent back to a place where she could find security.

Blood bonds are no longer sacred. The relationship of father-daughter or brother-sister is no more pure and sacred in today's world. Every single day, without fail, newspapers carry reports about a child being raped by a neighbour, daughters sexually molested by fathers, children working as "guest relations officers" — a euphemism for sex entertainers in disco houses and beer joints, children servicing the pleasure of the men in ships that dock in our ports and street children who are often at risk and vulnerable to prostitution and paedophilia.

Incidently, such cases are on the rise. Sita was a first class student and joined the M.B.B.S course at Madras Medical College. Her father would come every month to pay to the college the fees and looked like a caring father. Sita had lost her mother when she was a young girl. Since then her father would often visit hotels and restaurants with young girls. One day he booked himself at a well known South Indian Hotel in Chennai and came to the room drunk at about 11.00 P.M. The girl was waiting in the room and without even realising who the girl was he raped her. After some time, to his shock he realised, the girl he had raped was no one else but his daughter Sita. It was a tragic moment for both father and daughter and both of them committed suicide.

Nowadays, a girl is not even secure in her own house, what to mention about neighbours and impostors. Again, the perverse desires of men are responsible for such incidents along with the secondary status of girls in the society, and the scourge of illiteracy. Further, liquor adds to the problem of women hundredfold. When a man comes back home fully drunk he is unable to distinguish between his wife and daughter. He becomes very volatile and the victims are his wife and children especially daughters. This problem could be equally coupled with small dwelling units, large family size and less per capita income. In such a situation the responsibility of filling the deficiency falls on the woman.

Under such circumstances, the girl child becomes very vulnerable to the exploiters. She becomes an easy target for the traffickers. The menace of child prostitution has spread in our country like wildfire. It has engulfed our country as well as around the world. The plight of children is seen to be believed. Tourist places like Goa have turned into "Paedophiles' Paradise"; Mumbai's red-light areas are flooded with Nepali girls; Delhi's red-light area is equally inhabited by girls from all over India and neighbouring countries.

Conceding the magnitude of the problem I undertook the journey to nearly 394 districts in India for firsthand information as there was no records of proper data and research. The National Commission for Women sponsored countrywide studies on the subject in order to find out the magnitude and solutions on these difficult problems.

A survey done by the National Commission for Women shows that there are about 3 million prostitutes in India with 20 per cent or 600,000 of them minors. According to the Status of Action Report of the Central Advisory Board of India (1993), 15 per cent of all prostitutes are under the age of 15 and 24.5 per cent between the ages of 16 and 18. The report also claimed that about 70,000 -

1,00,000 prostitutes are in India's six main cities (Calcutta, Mumbai, Hyderabad, Bangalore, Chennai and Delhi). Ninety-four per cent are of them are Indians, 2.6 per cent are Nepalese and 2.7 per cent are Bangladeshi. At least 40,000 children are in prostitution in the six main cities alone. In an article entitled "India's ranking in terms of child prostitution on the rise" India has been rated to be at the top in the community of nations in terms of children engaged in prostitution. It is further stated that India has the inevitable distinction of having the largest number of children in prostitution in the world. Another article in the Delhi edition of *The Times of India* in Aug. 1996, observed that India's child flesh industry is considered the world's second largest, and recent estimates indicate that there were about 4,00,000 to 5,00,000 sex workers in India. According to NGOs the number is increasing by 8 - 10 per cent every year. The figures quoted by various organisations and studies vary. The exact statistical data about the magnitude of the male children involved in the trafficking is not available. However, it is contended that substantial proportion of male children too are engaged in this trade, causing deep national and international concern.

Though child prostitution is a term in popular usage, but it is not appropriate as it implies consent. And does the child ever give consent? This term refers to the sexual abuse and exploitation of children. It is perceived as the extreme form of violation of a child's body and mind within the context of child abuse and violence deliberately and purposefully aimed at a child.

Who is a Child?

In India, like in other countries, the definition of a child varies with the purpose. The Census of India treats persons below the age of 14 as 'Children'. While making use of standard demographic data, social scientists include females in the age group of 15-19 years under the category of the 'Girl Child'. According to the Constitution, no child below the age of 14 years shall be employed to work in any factory or mine or engaged in any other hazardous employment. Against the context of law the definition of the 'Child' depends very much upon the specific legislation. Then, it is an admixture of other terms, e.g. `juvenile', `minor', 'adolescent' and 'youth'. According to the Convention on the Rights of Child in 1990, in article I : the standard definition concerning a child is : " .... child means any human being below the age of 18, unless under the law applicable to the child, majority is attained earlier".

Indian law defines the "child" as an individual who is under the age of 16 years, and "minor" is one who is under the age of 18 years. For most of the Indians, sexual abuse of children is something thought to be a purely "western" term. On top of it, the term "Paedophilia" is alien altogether.

Let us begin with a review of the critical associations of our orthodox terms.

Minors-prostitution: This phrase institutionalises the abuse and forceful violation of the chastity of minors. "Minors in prostitution" alludes the phenomenal reality of adult women in prostitution a large proportion of whom are survivors of violence and abuse initiated during their childhood and youth.

But truth is often stranger than fiction. No matter how much we deny, the truth is that child prostitution has existed in our country and such crimes are increasing. With increasing tourism child prostitution is being practised at centres such as Puri and Paradeep ports in Orissa, Calcutta, Mangalore and Karwar in Karnataka, Cochin and Calicut in Kerala, Mamallapuram near Chennai and the famous beaches of Goa. The Centre of Concern for Child Labour (CCFCL) conducted a study in 1996 and warns that India has above 4 lakh under 15-year child prostitutes for child sex tourism alone. Thus, India has become number two after Thailand with 6 lakh child prostitutes. The founder of End Child Prostitution in Asian Tourism (ECPAT) Mr. Ron O' Grandy fears that India is becoming a replacement for other South Asian countries because of fewer laws against child sexual abuses.

An easy solution to the problem is of course that men stop seeking company of young girls. When a man goes out to 'deflower' a girl of 12 years he forgets that he has left behind a daughter of the same age at home. Why can't he place the two girls at par?

The above-mentioned facts lead us to focus on the "WHY" of child prostitution and trafficking? We need to look into the historical perspective, causes of child prostitution and trafficking. What is the role played by civic society? The role of the National Commission for Women and the Human Rights Commission is to ponder and reflect on how to rescue, rehabilitate and prevent this malaise affliciting our society.

2

Looking Back: The Historical Perspective

Prostitution and civilizations have gone hand in hand all over the world. Historically, religious beliefs and social customs prevalent in society from time to time provide the earliest accounts of its origin. It is rather difficult to enumerate or identify all the factors conducive to prostitution because it has often been argued that prostitution has its roots deep in the fabric of society.

India is no exception in spite of its spiritual aura. Therefore, it is important to trace the history of prostitution and sale of women to see how far practices in the past account for the position of women in present day society and reinforce toleration of assaults on the dignity of women by sexual violence and forced prostitution. The recorded Indian history indicates that prostitution was an accepted profession to which certain prerogatives, rights and duties were attached.

During the Brahmanic period prostitutes were called *Vaishyas* and it is conjectured that they were created to minister to the *Vaishya* or traders and merchants who led a life cut off for long periods of time from home and wives. (Basu & Sinha 1929; 22 29) It seems that it was from Egypt that legal prostitution found its way into India. The prostitutes were variously known as *Ganika, Bandhaki, Rupajiwa, Vaishya, Varangana, Kultani, Sambhali, Pumscali,* etc. Basu and Sinha (1925) felt that prostitution came to India from Egypt during the Brahmanic period and prostitutes were very much in existence during Mahabharata period.

In the sacred books of the Hindus, including the Ramayana and the Mahabharata, there are frequent references to prostitution. The kings on return to their kingdom were received by an escort of honour consisting of armies and Ganikas. Marriage with a prostitute was not looked down upon. The great Saint Vashist, was the son of a woman engaged in prostitution (*Vajrasuchi Upanishad*). The dancing girls were part of the court and were called *raja veshya* (royal prostitutes).

The great epics, besides giving an account of the high status and privileges that the Ganikas and courtesans enjoyed at that time also relate that degeneration had set in. The fact that prostitutes accompanied kings and his army in the battlefield implies women prostitutes could be taken wherever the soldiers wanted them for their sexual pleasure and even exposed to the danger of wars. They had become commodities and were taken to battlefields to satisfy the sexual desires of the soldiers.

With the resurgence of the Tantras in the medieval period, a new ethos for the socially vulnerable women comes to light. In the Shakta Tantras extreme sensitivity is shown to women. The Kaulavali Nirnaya (Chap. 21.96) unequivocally states that 'widows, low-caste women and prostitutes are worthy of respect'. The Paranand Tantra (16-17) equates 'a young, courtesan to Brahman; the Niruttara Tantra (Chap. 14), states that prostitutes are pure like holy places. This text outlines numerous ways in which they are to be honoured in the ritual of Shaktipuja.

During the Buddhist period, in spite of the adverse public opinion and punishments courtesans existed and commanded a certain amount of respect. They were accommodated in royal palaces, were highly paid and occupied a recognised position in the social scale. They even acquired a certain legendary distinction. Amrapali, the famous *hetaera* of Vissala existed in this period. Although prostitution was looked down by Jainism, no special stigma seems to have been attached to it. According to Jain sources, prostitution was so rampant in the country that Jain nuns were cautioned against it.

During Chandragupta Maurya's time (324-300 BC) the Greek envoy Megasthenes wrote that Amazons guarded the emperor's *harem* and formed the main bodyguard of the king. These women acted as a security force for the personal safety of the king. They were also efficient in the intelligent service of the king. Pataliputra was at this time the flourishing centre for prostitution, and it was probably for the first time that the attention of the state was drawn to a colony of prostitutes for its effective control and to bring it under the obligation of a stabilized taxation (Basu and Sinha, 1933; 202). The evidence of prostitution at this time comes from Kautilya, who wrote *Arthshastra* (321-296 BC). He used words such as *ganikas, prajniha, dasi, devadasi, rupadasi,* etc. for courtesans and prostitutes (Chandra Meti 1976; 64). Mauryan government appeared to have levied on each prostitute attached to the royal household, a tax amounting to two days' earnings per month or an equivalent of 7 per cent of her total monthly income.

During Ashoka's reign (272-232 BC) the superintendents of the royal *harem* and the courtesans were called Shri Adhykasha Mahanattas and their posts were maintained most likely till the seventh century AD. Vatsyan's *Kamasutra,* written probably in the early centuries of the Christian era (about 250-300 AD) is the most important source of information about courtesans and prostitutes in ancient India. According to Vatsyan the main causes of being courtesan in those days were desire for freedom, wealth' love and misfortune.

Shillapadikaram, written between 2nd and 5th century AD gives details of courtesans in South India. When Harsha ascended the throne (622 AD approximately), the traditional freedom and patronage of the dancing girls continued.

Kuvalayamala, written in 779 AD by Udyotanasuti at Jalod in Rajasthan is one of the books that gives a glimpse of courtesans of the medieval times. The system of attaching prostitutes to places of worship is of ancient origin, but it seems to have come into regular practice during the ninth and tenth centuries when the ritual in the temples attained the present form.

The destruction of great temples by Muslim invaders and erection of mosques in the place of temples was the beginning of the decline of the Devadasi system in North India, whereas in South India which was ruled by Hindu Rajas, the institution flourished with the same vigour as it did in pre-Muslim India. The rulers who followed Krishnadeva Raya were incompetent with the result Vijayanagar gradually declined in power. Polygamy, sati and child marriage were common.

In the Mughal period (1526-1787AD) prostitution was a recognized institution, but among Muslims prostitution was the antithesis to the institution of family life and while the singing and dancing girls who practised it became rich and even powerful they were never treated as part of society, as they had been in earlier times.

Emperor Akbar (1556-1605 AD) made some regulations so that the services of the prostitutes might not be available very easily to the public. Prostitutes were confined to a place outside the capital city which was known as Shaitanpura or the devil's quarters. A register was maintained outside Shaitanpura for every client who enters into the *Shaitanpura* to sign his name and address. The next morning the register was presented to the Emperor. With this innovative method the clientele at Shaitanpura dwindled.

Emperor Shahjahan (1627-1657 AD) reviewed the activities once again. When Aurangzeb became the ruler, most of his rules were directed towards prohibition of prostitutes. In spite of many regulations imposed by the Mughal emperors like Akbar and Aurangzeb, prostitution received great encouragement from the rich and well-to-do sections of the people.

The coming of European power (in the 15th century) to India, especially the English, played an important role in bringing about the downfall of the Mughal Empire on the one hand and on the other efforts were made to cater to the sexual needs of the soldiers based in India, "a practice although against the British norms in the native country!" British army authorities maintained special brothels called Chaklas in the nineteenth century. Although they discouraged the sati system, class hatred, child marriage, purdah system nevertheless female education and remarriage of widows were encouraged and laws dealing with immoral traffic were enacted. However in many provinces official police registers were kept, for the convenience of the police " to keep an eye on the anti-social elements who usually frequented the brothels".

Forms and Names

In ancient times names given to prostitutes were varied and as per to the duties assigned to them. For instance prostitutes who served nobility were called *ganikas,* and were well versed in the arts; *Ganikaadheksha* was superintendent of prostitutes; *Pratiganika* was substitute prostitute employed for a short term period during absence of *ganika; Punschal* was low grade prostitute; *Kritavardha* and *Avarudha* were professional prostitutes who lived as mistress and under the protection of one master. The profession of prostitution was state managed and the prostitutes besides providing sexual services to the citizens and nobility also acted as spies to keep a watch on the enemies, thieves and other anti-state elements.

Vatsyayan classified prostitutes into *Ganika* at the top, *Kulata,* (married woman involved with other men), *Paricharika* a mistress in the house of nobles and *Kumbhadasi* as the lowest category of prostitutes. During the eighteenth and nineteenth century *Nautch* girls (or the dancing girls or *baijees)* became very popular in providing recreation and sensual pleasures to the rich and resourceful people in India, specially in Bengal province. Joardar had mentioned three types of prostitutes in his study in Calcutta city, namely, (1) *Chukli* lower category of prostitute who provides food and shelter in lieu of her services; (2) *Adia* — a prostitute who gets half of her income. In both the cases *Mashi* or female brothelkeeper takes charge of the income; and (3) Self-employed or independent prostitute—she is her own *mashi.*

In 1923, the Suppression of Immoral Traffic Act (SITA) was passed for Calcutta, Madras and Bombay Presidencies which followed suit. In UP, the Naik Girls Protection Act (Millet Kate, *The Prostitution Papers,* 1971, quoted in Maby Gibson op. cit.) and Minor Girls' Protection Act were passed in 1923. Attempts at abolition of brothels began after the passing of these Acts.

After independence, more systematic attention has been paid to this problem. Both preventive and curative aspects of the problem have been taken up for policy formulation and implementation. An Advisory Committee on Social and Moral Hygiene was set up by the Central Social and Welfare Board in

1954 to review the existence of this profession all over India.

The Suppression of Immoral Traffic in Women and Girls Act (SITA) was passed by Parliament in 1956 and amended in 1986 as the Prevention of Immoral Traffic in Women and Girls Act (ITPA).

The use of prostitutes as an organised system by the army may have disappeared by the end of nineteenth century but traditional prostitution, both religious and common, continued to flourish. Kate Millet, a legal aid advisor in America has written: "The actual situation in the city is that prostitution is accepted by everyone—the police, judge, clerk and lawyers. Arrest and prosecution are purely gestures that have to be made to keep up the facade of public morality. The method of dealing with it is simply a form of harassment not a form of prevention, abolition or punishment...only a total and satisfied acceptance of the double standard, excusing the male, accusing the female. Though, Millet had described this situation for America, the same applies for almost all the countries, India being no exception.

Mahatma Gandhi had once stated that: "It is a matter of bitter shame and sorrow and of deep humiliation that a number of women have to sell their chastity for men's lust. Man, the law-giver, will have to pay a dreadful penalty for the degradation he has imposed upon the so-called weaker sex. When woman, freed from man's snares, rises to the full height and rebels against man's legislation and institution, designed by him, her rebellion, no doubt non-violent, will be nonetheless effective".

Some research studies suggested the factors to be conducive to prostitution as destitution; desertion, neglect, ill-treatment; strained relation, deception, bad influences, illegitimate pregnancy, illicit sexual relations, ignorance, sex curiosity, sexual urge, desire for easy life, desire for revenge, industrialisation, urbanisation, tradition, hereditary, prohibiting of widow remarriage and adopting double standards for men and women whereby men are allowed considerable sexual freedom and women ostracised on the score of chastity.

The studies on prostitutes reveals that most of the women/

girls in this profession have not taken up this work by their own choice, rather they have been pushed into it involuntarily. From this account it is clear that in most cases prostitution is not a moral problem. First of all, an economic problem, a social dilemma, it is a psychological predicament. Moreover, the present Indian society and for that matter any society reflects a sick male society which is obsessed with male chauvinism and perversion. And this has resulted in increasing the problem of prostitution.

Research Findings

Various studies have revealed that prostitutes belong to different categories enumerated as follows:

Street walker

These are prostitutes who function independently or through pimps. They have no security and no support to combat the pimps and are time and again exploited economically, emotionally and sexually either by clients or others.

Cage brothel prostitutes

This is a unique practice reported from around Mumbai. Such prostitutes are attached to a brothel, which has a landlord who in turn rents the premises to a brothelkeeper. The brothelkeeper runs the brothel and appoints a manager who supervises and keeps a watch on all the women, pimps, procurers and henchmen. The caged prostitutes are basically minors, below 18 years of age. Their earnings may range between Rs. 50-100 per day which is pocketed by the brothelkeeper till such time the brothelkeeper's investment made in procuring her has been recovered. The brothelkeepers do not release these girls as long as they get regular and rich clients. Young girls and virgins are very much in demand and therefore their earnings during the earlier years are high. (Pai Patker, pp. 11-12)

Brothel prostitutes

These are women who practise prostitution in brothels or brothel-like outfits under the rules and regulations of the brothels set by people managing the same. The women are dependent on brothelkeepers, pimps, etc. and provide sexual favours to their clients in exchange of money. A good amount of their earning is shared among various categories of persons including brothelkeeper, pimps, etc. Their earnings may vary from Rs. 10-50 per client. These prostitutes belong to low socio-economic group families. The number of clients they entertain daily is quite high and the localities where the brothels are situated are either densely populated or have high frequency of floating population, e.g. G.B. Road (Delhi), Kamathipura (Mumbai), Khidirpur, Sonagachi, (Calcutta), etc.

Singing and dancing girls

Under this category the girls normally start by singing and dancing for clients and may end with sexual favours. It is important to mention that these women are not entirely dependent on prostitution. They have some degree of freedom in terms of practising prostitution. They are drawn from lower to middle class groups. Most of the time they operate from prostitution prone areas or from brothels.

A girl named Rashida with long black hair and dusky complexion, huge big eyes, now 21 years old whom I had met at Chaturbujstan, in Muzaffarpur district, Bihar narrated the following account:

She said when she was three years old she found herself following her mother everywhere curious to know what her mother was doing. The girl said that by the time she knew who she was, her mother Roshan Devi sent her off to school from 6 a.m. to 8 p.m. She said that she would never disclose at the school that she was from the red-light area of Chaturbhujstan. She has five sisters and three brothers. In the school whenever the children would ask for her home address she would give a wrong address. However, many times her friends would insist on visiting her home and she would always avoid that due to embarrassment and stigma. Once, through a friend of her's who was also going to school with her from the red-light area, the address and whereabouts of the friend somehow became known to the other girls at the school and they would taunt her. Seeing her friend's condition made her cringe and feel always insecure, afraid that her identity may also be disclosed. She does not know who her father was. Life was an uncertainty and a heavy burden. Once her real father sent his sons asking if they could assist in her marriage, but she refused to go. They were rich people from Begusarai. She told me: "Ma, all the little girls want to get good education, want to go to school and live with happiness". Rashida told us that now she has passed 12th class, she lives in the area where child prostitution is rampant day and night although she hates the profession, but tomorrow if she does not get a job she will have no other alternative but to fall back on her mother's profession!

Barmaids

A few of the barmaids indulge in prostitution after the bar is closed.

Theatre / Cinema girls

A special category of prostitutes reported in the Bombay study are those who give 'company' to men and accompany them to cinema halls. They do not necessarily indulge in sexual activities except when some men take them to hotels for the purpose after watching movies. In such situations these women earn a little extra money.

Massage parlours and health centre attendants

These girls start with massaging or exercising or checkups and land up with sexual favours. They either work in this set-up on full time or part-time basis or work through these set-ups. These girls as well as their clients belong to middle and upper class income groups. Hence, the income of this group is also high.

The *Delhi Times* on Friday, 19th June, 1998 brought out "the thriving business of massage parlours in the capital". It says:

"But it clearly isn't the massage alone which brings in the money. Masquerading as gigolos, masseurs in the city who advertise themselves as 'health clubs and physical fitness professionals,' openly provide services for women which go well beyond a simple massage. One such "available" young man, speaking fluent English, wanted Rs. 3,000, in addition to dinner and drinks at a five-star hotel. He said he was 21, 5 feet 11 inch in height and had a great body. To top it all, he described himself as an Anil Kapoor look-alike. "If I'm in the mood, we could even check in for the entire night. I won't charge you extra – consider it a discount," he said. The other services include a massage by one, two and even three "handsome" young boys, with a 45-minute to one-hour session costing Rs. 500. This could include "anything that you want," besides the mandatory massage. To top it all, they offer "complete confidentiality," and take pains to reassure the caller, "Your husband would never know, if that is what you are afraid of." Massage parlours are not a new phenomenon in the capital and have been around for years but, as the advertisements suggest, have taken on new dimensions only in the past few years. The target invariably is the neglected housewife, the single women tired of a humdrum existence, looking for some adventure." One of the parlours contacted by *Delhi Times* even had provision for a child-room! Some of these parlours are located in posh South Delhi colonies such as Hauz Khas, Defence Colony and Lajpat Nagar but several are also located in the far-flung areas of Rohini, Rajouri Garden and Rajendra Nagar.

Independently operating prostitutes

These normally belong to lower and lower middle class groups of families and mostly serve the clients of the same group. The majority of them work without pimps. They are found in highly congested areas of big cities, like slums, resettlement colonies, etc. Most of them are working women who resort to prostitution regularly or intermittently as a means of supplementing their monthly incomes.

Call girls

This phenomenon is of recent origin. Most of the girls of this category belong to upper middle class families. They may own an apartment with telephone and other amenities wherein they practise the profession. Generally, they go out to posh hotels and most of the times stay in posh colonies of the city for the purpose of prostitution. They may operate independently or through a contact/manager. Some of them may have regular clients who may be willing to pay higher fees for exclusive services. They too, share their income with their contacts.

(Report of the Fifth All India Conference on Moral and Social Hygiene, 1956; p. 24.)

3

Traditional Forms of Prostitution : Prostitution in Places of Worship

Unlike call girls, prostitution associated with religion has been an age-old phenomenon. The female dancer and singers attached to temples are generally referred to by the term "Devadasi" which literally means "female slaves of the deity". Their dedication to temple service is considered as constituting a marriage with the deity. The cult of dedicating girls to the temple is prevailing all over India in different forms and names, such as *Devadasis* in Karnataka, *Maharis* in Kerala, *Natis* in Assam, *Murlis* in Maharashtra, *Bogams, Jogalis/ Jogins* and *Basavis* in Andhra Pradesh, *Thevardiyer* in Tamil Nadu and *Bhavins* in Goa.

These servants of deities were said to be expert in music and dance in the medieval period. As centuries passed, their services shifted from gods to earthly gods and lords. The women so dedicated to the deity as Devadasis, usually lead a life of prostitute with a religious sanction. This type of organised system has different rural manifestations, as mentioned above, but all systems demand initiation into prostitution by puberty at the latest. Also, rural child prostitution is rooted in the continued exploitation of the scheduled castes and the position of girls is the most oppressed within these historically oppressed groups.

Many a time the young girls of low castes, even before the onset of puberty, are singled out by the rich or powerful people of the community or by the parents themselves. The person who is the highest bidder, finances the dedication ceremony with much fanfare. The whole community is invited to take part in this ceremony and the little girl is marked as devadasi or jogin or bhavin, etc. On attainment of puberty the person who had financed the dedication ceremony "deflowers" the girls. The girl is attached to this person till the time he wishes to keep her. Once the man curtails the relation she is attached to another person by the priest or family head. These women are not supposed to accept or demand any money from the man. They are also forbidden to marry any mortal man. Thus, these women are constantly under threat of exploitation and lead a life of sexual slavery. In short, the dedication ceremony is a licence for prostitution with religious sanction which pushes the girl into this profession for a lifetime. The characteristics of various forms of this culture is shown further on.

Devadasi System

This system exists in Andhra Pradesh, Maharashtra, and Karnataka. The sites of most intense Devadasi activity are located in a belt on either side of the Karnataka/Maharashtra border: Belgaum, Dharwar, Bijapur and Gulbarga in Karnataka and Tagnagiri, Satara, Kolhapur, Solapur and Osmanabad in Maharashtra. Men and women dedicate themselves in the service of Goddess Yellamma and are called Jogayya (Devadasi) and 'jagati' respectively. The temple of Yellamma is situated in Athani Taluka of Belgaum district. Girls are dedicated to Yellamma goddess on full moon day of Chaitra (March-April) or Magha (Nov-Dec.) months at temples of Saundatti or Kokatnur on a mass scale (the number of girls being dedicated may vary from 1000 to 5000). Contemporary Devadasis are not supported by these temples in return for their dancing and singing. Hence, a number of Devadasis resort to prostitution, as prescribed by the tradition to earn their living.

Most of the girls belonging to Devadasi group are from Mahar, Mang, Dowani and Chambhar Scheduled Castes groups. Their families are trapped by poverty and often depend upon the income supplied by their daughters, the income being funneled down to them from the higher caste, wealthier men who can pay for the services of a prostitute.

Girls are dedicated to the goddess not only at the behest of rich people but also due to a number of other reasons such as: lack of son; too many daughters in the family; mother being in the profession, elder sister or any other member of the family being a Devadasi; manifestation of the 'signs' that designate a girl destined for the goddess such as matted, dry hair, white patch; eczema, leprosy and mental retardation have been traditionally interpreted as sign of the call of goddess Yellamma. Some of the families create these signs artificially to gain religious sanction for their need or desire to profit from their daughter's earnings as a prostitute.

As mentioned earlier, most of the times the dedication ceremony is financed by a wealthy man and after attainment of puberty this person has the right to the girl's virginity. At the time of 'deflowering' the man pay's a lump sum money to the girl's family. Hence, the financial returns to the family of girl are immediate, and they profit from her earnings as long as she continues to work. A Devadasi family also receive regular gifts of presents and cash on those specific days dedicated to the goddess Yelamma from caste Hindus who worship this goddess.

Since the past two years, the National Commission for Women has been working on the rehabilitation of Devadasis, child prostitution, Muttangis and prostitutes. Last year, I visited Belgaum, Athni, Soudatti, Gokak and discovered that majority of the Devadasis had given up their profession but no publicity was given for the same. The Media, both Indian and foreign, have been portraying the Devadasi system as if it is the biggest problem in India. To my surprise, these 2000 strong women who are no longer Devadasis, are not only getting a livelihood from various vocations, but are also preventing other children from entering into the system. To highlight this, the National Commission for Women requested the Karnataka State Commission for Women to organise a Devadasi meet at Bangalore. The NCW financially supported this meet at Bangalore. It was indeed a sight worth seeing where 500 Devadasis assembled together to tell how they have changed their lives and how they have become agents of change. For two days we heard various women describing to us some of their achievements and problems. Their main problems were:

(i) housing;

(ii) education for their children;
(iii) marriage of their daughters and many a time themselves;
(iv) guarantee of employment as soon as they give up the profession.

The women were vocal and spoke about the good work that was being done by Ms Lata, the women and child project incharge in bringing about this change. Swami Taralbala was very kind in giving his premises for the conference. I was a little disappointed that when such agents of change are talking about empowerment and progress, the Press was not there to show this marked improvement in society. It is a sad reflection that the press only carries sensational news. Justice Krishna Iyer delivered the valedictory address at the Devadasis Meet.

Specific Recommendations on Prostitution through Religious Sanction:

1. Rules should immediately be formulated to back-up the decade-old legislation in this regard. The village panchayats should be held responsible in case of dedication of girls as Devadasis and to a life of prostitution.

2. With the devolution of powers to the panchayats and also conferring upon them financial automony, the panchayats should be responsible for educating the children of the existing Devadasis.

3. Land reforms should confer land deeds on the Devadasis, a majority of whom are landless labourers employed in the trade of prostitution to augment there earnings. The panchayats must ensure that there are no benami transactions and that the Devadasis are the rightful owners of the land allotted to them.

4. In view of the tardy implementation of the Devadasi Act, there is need to have a monitoring agency with the specific task of liaising with various agencies involved in the implementation of the Act. The agency so formed should have adequate representation from the non-governmental

organizations who have been engaged in working with the Devadasis. The monitoring agency should submit periodic reports and the feedback thus obtained should be taken as input for improving the efficiency of the system.

5. The rehabilitation programmes suffer from a few inadequacies that need to be rectified. These are:
   - that programmes should not be time-bound. Short duration programmes are inadequate for finding long-term solutions to the problem at hand;
   - the marketing arrangements for the products prepared by the by Devadasis are quite inadequate. Assured marketing channels have to be provided to the Devadasis in order that the rehabilitation schemes become viable avenues for earning and livelihood;
   - the programmes have to be taken up at a much bigger scale than exists at present. For strengthening their rehabilitation larger participation of NGOs should be ensured.

6. Most of the women have expressed their desire to get educated but the literacy programmes have not taken off in any of the endemic areas. An overwhelming number of Devadasis want to educate their children, but poverty coupled with social stigma, has ensured low levels of enrolment in schools and high drop-out rates. Integrated schools for children of Devadasis, is an option that can be considered.

7. Finally a detailed census of the Devadasi population in Karnataka, Andhra Pradesh, Orissa and Rajasthan must be conducted immediately to help in getting the right numbers of such women, and to understand the conditions in which they live. The last detailed census conducted in Belgaum was in 1986 and those statistics are not relevant to the present situation.

8. The need is currently for a Central legislation to check

prostitution through religious sanction or tradition, so that in all states where such practices are prevalent, necessary action can be initiated.

Basavi System

This system, being much less organised than the Devadasi system both religiously and financially, is made possible by the same social realities of poverty and gender discrimination. This system is known to exist in the slums of Secunderabad, Bellary, Raichur, Gulbarga and Chitradurga districts of Andhra Pradesh. "Basavi" means "female bull" which ostensibly connotes the bull's freedom to wander. Historically, Basavis were forbidden to marry and spent their lives performing religious duties for God Hanuman.

Like the Devadasi system, Basavis also come from Scheduled Caste families both poor and uneducated, and believe that religion will fulfil their economic needs and/or wants. They, too, feel that a daughter can be sacrificed, if her initiation into the Basavi system might cause a deity to look kindly on them, granting them a son or relief from costly medical bills or a generally bright future.

Under this system too, girls are dedicated at pre-puberty age to number of deities, the most important of which is goddess Yellamma. Matted hair are again 'signs' for dedication. She undergoes a ceremony with Hindu priests in a temple and then, dressed in a white saree, she is given ceremonial jewellery and begging baskets. The Basavis do not immediately enter into lifelong careers as prostitutes, in fact this tradition still demands the performance of certain ritual duties. Using the begging baskets bestowed upon them at their dedication ceremony Basavis must beg continuously for three days during certain ritual days and they must also worship the goddess Yellamma at least twice a week. Basavis usually turn to prostitution as begging does not usually generate sufficient income.

The Jogin System

This is another form of religious, rural prostitution that automatically qualifies as child prostitution and is based on the oppression of the Scheduled. Castes by the upper castes and the oppression of girls within families. This form of prostitution is endemic to Andhra Pradesh and in the north- western districts of the Telangana region, viz. Nizamabad, Adilabad, Karimnagar and Medak.

In this system also girls are "married" to a god before puberty and enter prostitution when they reach puberty. Like most Scheduled Caste communities, the ones who practise the Jogin tradition are impoverished to the point that daily survival is often a struggle. Economic need is a necessary prerequisite for a system that functions mainly to supply wealthy men in the region with a convenient source of prostitutes. Since the daughters of these families are powerless to oppose their parents' wishes, they are usually exploited as a source of income by initiating them into the Jogin system.

Often, a wealthy person in the region will select a young girl who appeals to him and will request that her family "marry" her to the village deity. At times, the family might marry the girl to the god in order to appease him after some display of divine displeasure. The sponsor of the ceremony loans the family money to pay for the ritual feast at the dedication ceremony, which occurs when the girl is 10 years old. At puberty, girl undergoes a second ceremony, after which the man who has paid for the dedication has the right to sleep with her first.

The Jogin is, thereafter, condemned to a life of prostitution, which often does not generate enough money for mere survival and they must also find other labour, usually of a manual nature. The Jogin also has religious duties, such as dancing around corpses and dancing on certain festival days. Social ostracism and public humiliation are commonly inflicted by the rural population on the Jogins when they are obligated to dance in public.

Bogams

These are women attached to the temples of Shiva and Vishnu as "Servants of Gods" in and around areas of Hyderabad. They earn their living by dancing, singing and prostitution. Bogams are both Hindus and Mohmmedans. Hindu Bogams are known as *sani, nayaka* and Muslim Bogams are titled as *jan, nayakan.*

Bogam Sani are married to the idol of Lord Krishna at the initiation ceremony and Bogam Jan are Married to a dagger. In the former case a marriage booth of sixteen pillars is put up at the girl's house, where the idol is brought on an auspicious day. The girl is made to stand before the idol as if it were the bridegroom, a curtain is held between them and the officiating Brahmin, reciting the *Mangal ashtaka,* or marriage stanzas, weds them in the orthodox fashion. On the Nagveli day the girl is seated by the side of the idol and worships Gauri, the consort of Shiva. Betel leaves, nuts and kumkum are distributed to the assembly of dancing girls. The girls are taught to sing and dance at the early age of seven or eight, so that they are able to perform at the age of twelve or thirteen and then continue to dance till the age of thirty or forty. They dance daily before the idols, while the priests are officiating and offering puja to them. The majority of them are trained to appear in public, when they are profusely ornamented with gold and jewels and sumptuously dressed in silk and muslin.

Bhavins

Bhavins are found in Goa and the Konkan region as well as in Bombay. They are engaged in service of Lord Mangesh in Goa and in the temples of Lord Ganesh in Mumbai. Some of these women are presented to god in infancy by their parents. Girls turn "Bhavins" by simply pouring oil on their heads from the god's lamp. On attaining puberty the girl is formally married and thereafter practises prostitution promiscuously.

Murlis

Murlis are girls dedicated to God Khandoba, believed to be the incarnation of Lord Shiva, in Maharashtra. The girls are dedicated to God in early infancy by their parents. Kumbis, Mahars, Mangs and other low castes make Murlis of their daughter, mostly because of economic strain. High caste people though visit Jejuri (headquarters of God Khandoba) near Pune, never offer their own girls but buy girls of low caste for small amounts of money to offer to God. which is not a very difficult job. Murlis, after being married to God Khandoba at puberty are forbidden to marry any other man, and as a result, usually lead an infamous life earning a livelihood by sin. Some of these girls become wandering Murlis.

Others become ordinary public women in any town or city; while a few are said to live for years with one man. The parents of such girls do not feel ashamed to take her earnings, because they belong to Khandoba and what they do is not sin in the eyes of his devotees.

Prostitution in Tribal Societies

In this category, centuries ago tribes organized themselves around the system of prostitution that almost completely disempowers the daughters of those tribes mainly because of economic and social marginalization. Like most forms of religious prostitution the tribal system automatically fall under the category of child prostitution, since they mandate that their girls be initiated by puberty at the latest. It is practised by Banchara and Bedia Tribes in Madhya Pradesh, various tribes in Rajasthan and the Domare tribe in Andhra Pradesh. Many of these tribes are now classified among the Scheduled Castes.

Bedia Tribe

During my visits to Madhya Pradesh I had the opportunity of visiting the Bedia tribe or Bedni tribe where most womenfolk in their childhood are engaged in singing, dancing and prostitution.

The historic roots of prostitution practised by these tribes demonstrate that prostitution can easily become the last resort response of a group to economic marginalization. These tribes, who traditionally served the princely armies of their region, turned to criminal activity, when the advent of British rule dispersed the armies and robbed the tribes of their livelihood. (Harsh-Mander) The British often imprisoned the tribal men for long periods of time with or without any actual justification and to earn a livelihood the womenfolk turned to prostitution. The men only showed resistance initially but over time accepted it for the easy money and gradually, the only means of survival developed into the rigid tradition of social organisation. The women became the principal earners of the family whereas the males either solicit clients for their daughters, sisters, mothers or engage in petty criminal activities or remain idle. This development deprived most of the girls and women involved of their right to make a decision about their lives.

The mother of any girl has to declare during her childhood itself in the presence of the village deity "Narsima" (folk form of Durga) whether she will introduce her daughter into prostitution or give her in marriage. The initiation of daughter into prostitution is an occasion for celebration. It is a mandatory caste rule that at least one daughter in each family be reserved for prostitution. A married woman is fully debarred from the profession of prostitution. On the other hand, the prostitute is debarred from having sexual relations with anyone of the community. All these caste rules are believed to have divine sanction and their contravention invites severe penalties and social boycott.

Interestingly the Bedia man did not usually marry. His mother or sister would bring a dancer woman from some other caste to make the family complete to avoid the possibility of the dancing wife coming in contact with some other persons. The Bedias devised a novel tradition under which the Bedia wife would never dance and remain a faithful wife. This brings us to the right definition – "Bedni is one who sings and dances and is engaged in prostitution but a Bedia's wife is not a Bedni".

Bednis are known as the main exponents of a very popular dance form of Bundelkhand called Rai. Rai is culturally a rich art form but has come into disrepute because of the association of prostitution with it. Rai is a group song and dance item in which there are five or six male singers and instrument players with one or two female dancers. One night's programme costs Rs. 2,000/- to 3,000/- and the players are generally men from higher castes. It may be interesting to mention here that most of the Bedia people have traditional vocations—agriculture, animal husbandry, etc. But it is still not their main livelihood. The male folk without any scruples enjoy the income brought home by their sisters and mothers. The relationship of brother and sister remains present in the children born of a mother but the emotional bond is never strong because the brother is not very sure that the sister is from his own father.

However the scene of yesteryears has changed drastically. The stirrings of change among the two communities, which subsists in the shadow of rural society in several regions and even in some

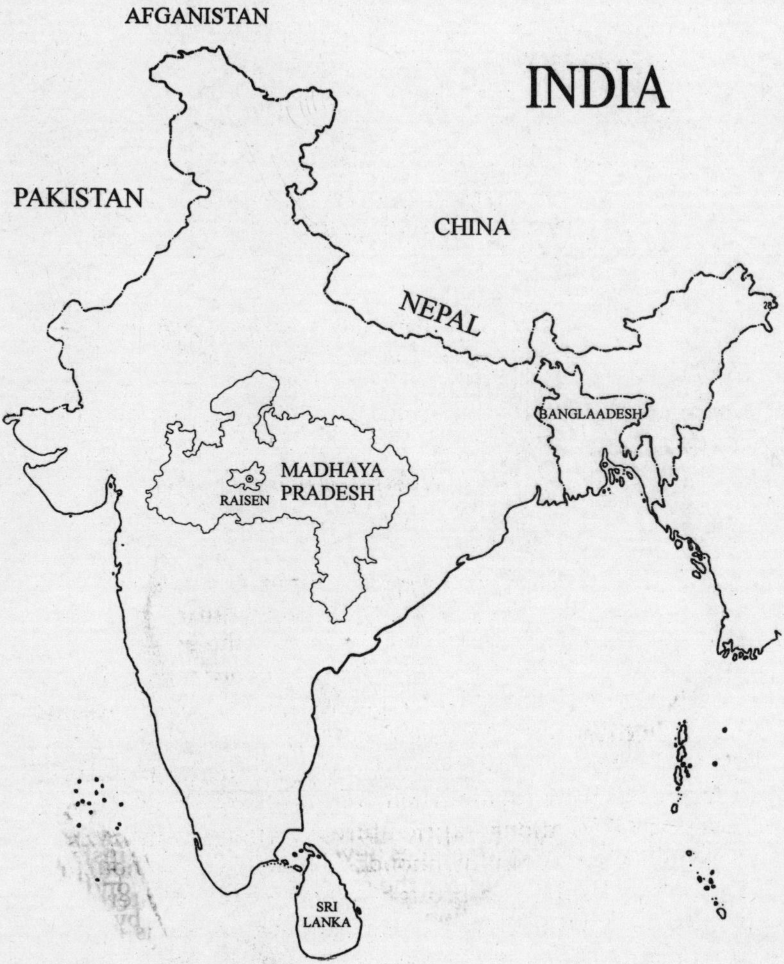

AFGANISTAN
INDIA
PAKISTAN
CHINA
NEPAL
BANGLAADESH
MADHAYA
PRADESH
RAISEN
SRI
LANKA

towns, are still not strong enough to develop into a convincing movement for the transition of these communities into the national mainstream.

Our visit to the Ashram in Morena run by Shri Ram Snehi gave insight into a new dimension to the Bedia tribe. Shri Ram Snehi has set up "Jabali Yochana" for the girlchild of Bedia community. We met girls from the Bedia community who were rescued from prostitution and educated. We found 200 girls performing Karate and self-defence exercises. These girls are a sign of hope that they are being loved and cared. So was the case during our visit to Pathariya village in Sagar district. Champa Behn, a disciple of Acharya Vinoba Bhave had invited us to the group marriage ceremony of many of the Bedia girls who had been living in her Ashram since childhood. It was a novel and brilliant effort to bring about change for the betterment of the Bedia community. She had so far performed 900 collective marriages on *Basant Panchami* and they take a pledge on that day to end prostitution. Since 1984 Champa Behn has prevented Bedia girls in Pathariya turning into Bednis. Boys and girls of this community are being educated and learning skills are imparted. Shri Ram Snehi, Champa Behn and many other spoke about the evil effects of liquor, and the resulting family environment that made these little girls a prey to sex abuse. Many rich Bedia men also accept prostitution as a source of income.

We were shocked to see that little girls aged only eight were also settling a price with their customers. While the Bedia men without any shame under the pretext of the tradition would let their young daughters go, the fathers told us that they were not sure if the child belonged to them. Hence, the custom is that Bedia girl gets her mother's name instead of the father's.

Though much has been done for the rehabilitation of this community, however, much more needs to be done.

The Banchara Tribe

The Bancharas are mainly found in the districts of Mandsaur, Ujjain, Indore, Shahjapur and Ratlam, whereas the Bedia tribe is spread out over 16 districts but are concentrated in Guna, Sagar,

Morena, Panna, Shivpuri, Vidisha, Rajgarh and Raisen. The 1981 census had shown that 47 per cent of the Banchara women and 44 per cent of the Bedia women are unmarried. This can be presumed to be roughly the proportion of women engaged in prostitution in these two castes. There is no material available to deduce the number of girls under 18 involved in the profession.

Marrige is an extremely difficult problem for Banchara and Bedia men, and they have to seek out girls of other communities or orphaned and abandoned girls. In both communities the practice of giving very high bride price is prevalent, owing to shortage of bride, reinforcing the system of prostitution. This is because the families which have withdrawn from prostitution usually no longer afford the bride price, whereas those still in trade are economically much more sound and can afford the bride price to bring home the most eligible brides.

It is difficult to generalize about the economic status of the Bancharas and Bedias. They span much of the economic spectrum, ranging from those engaged in urban prostitution with high incomes and a visible upper middle class consumerist lifestyles to the very poor, landless, highway rural prostitutes. There are several instances of women being purchased for red-light areas in the metropolises, or as mistresses. In some cases, groups of Bedia women have even travelled abroad for prostitution and have returned with very substantial incomes. Bedia families in Morena for instance possess expensive consumer durables like cars, VCRs, refrigerators, etc. Women adopted as mistresses by rural rich enjoy greater economic security, but this practise is becoming rare and is being replaced by casual prostitution. On the other extreme, there are rural settlements of such prostitutes who live in very sparse hutments with few household goods, little economic security and can barely sustain their family.

The social status of the women within the family is complex. There is no doubt that because the woman is the principal bread-winner, she enjoys a comparative degree of freedom, independence and control within her family and social set-up that is not found in other caste groups. There being no taboo against prostitution, the social status of women practising prostitution is often higher than that of married women.

The Rajnat Tribe

This tribe's history of prostitution stretches back further than that of the Bancharas and Bedias. They have always been consigned to the role of prostitutes by the upper castes. The only difference in their condition then and today is that when they served the Rajput royalty, they were given money and land as payment. When the royalty could no longer afford to patronize the Rajnats, the tribe settled itself in villages along the major roads of Rajasthan, especially along the highways running through the Alwar district and have practised prostitution there since that time.

The historical plight of the lower castes, then translated itself into this tribe's contemporary situation. The Rajnats are similar to the Bancharas and Bedias in two important ways: the tribal organisation is such that it robs the girls of the freedom of choice concerning their own lives, and their underlying economic powerlessness forces the tribe into prostitution. Each first daughter born into the family is expected to contribute by carrying on the traditional profession as soon as she reaches the puberty, and no girl is able to raise her head against this trend.

The social organisation of the tribe is demonstrative of the oppression of the tribe itself and of the females within it. The only difference between similar tribes is a relatively superficial one that women instead of men are in control. In the Rajnat village of Kukubaas, e.g., the name of the village, which means "Kukus house", indicates clearly who is in charge. The village, in fact, was named after the current Kuku's mother; the name exerts the power of these woman who were both prostitutes and the village leaders. The woman who is at the helm today oversees the village's business of prostitution. It is woman such as she in the different villages who run the auction of the initiation ceremony, where the highest bidder purchases the girl's virginity as well as sexual right to her for the rest of her life without any payment to the victim.

Once a girl has been initiated she reports to the kuku of her village, who makes sure that the prostitutes are regularly placing themselves along the roadside to attract the desired number of 15 clients a day per girl. In Kukubaas it is she who sets the rate, which is normally Rs. 20 per client. She halves the rate, however, when business is slack. She also directs the men of the village, whose responsibility is to solicit clients in neighbouring towns. The client pool of Rajnat tribe is less indicative of the historic caste inequalities that feed other systems of rural prostitution. Their clients are only occasionally drawn from the classes of rural landowners. More often, they are merchants or farmers doing business in nearby towns, or truckers passing through the area. As Rajnat tribe is close to Delhi, they frequently receive clients in cars as some urban businessmen. This proximity has, however, increased the demand for younger girls. A girl's first night may cost as much as one lakh. The demand for younger girls is again the result of belief that they can cure the sexually transmitted diseases or that at least they will not transmit them.

The Dommara Tribe

The Dommara tribe is spread in the tribal region of the Telengana districts : Warangal, Nizamabad, Medak, Karimnagar and Nalgonda, in Andhra Pradesh. This tribe also initiates its girls into prostitution at puberty and sets an example for prostitution based gender oppression within the community. Dommara prostitutes are known as "Venkatasanis". The historical ostracism suffered by tribal communities has resulted in the durability of the tradition, which stretches back hundreds of years. It carries on, however, partially because the cruel nature of the tradition has destroyed the prostitute's powers of resistance. The tribe has a vested interest in maintaining it as it is benefitted from the system. The oldest daughter is inducted into the tradition who becomes the main source of income for the family. She even pays for her younger brothers' and sisters' marriage.

The brutality of the Dommara system manifests itself even before the girl's initiation. Girls who will become "Venkatasanis" are often subjected to sexual abuse from family and villagers right up to their time of initiation ceremony at puberty. At that point, they go through a ceremony that is typical in that they are bathed in turmeric and married to the village deity. However, these girls are then forced to submit to group sex with village leaders and priests within the temple for a full week while her family and the rest of the village feast and celebrate.

Some of the girls have reportedly died of injuries and shock sustained during this experience; the ones who survive must thereafter serve as paid prostitutes for men of the tribe. She resides as well as receives customers in her family's hut until she is 20 and then receives her own dwelling. Despite the fact that her earnings support her family, the practising Venkatasani is generally ostracised by them, as well as by the community generally. In Warangal and Nizamabad districts, there are actually whole villages composed exclusively of Venkatsanis. During our visit to Warangal we had the opportunity of visiting some of the Venkatasanis and found them to be living in a comfortable lifestyle patronized by rich clients.

Halvagal Village

Halvagal village observes yet another form of rural prostitution that is borne most strikingly out of the economic marginalization of the Scheduled Castes. The Halvagal village is located in the Bellary district in Karnataka. The girls of this village are inducted into the system from ages 12 to 15. They may be numerically insignificant in the context of child prostitution throughout India but they are important because their plight indicates that the disparities between the castes in rural areas can lead to isolated pockets of organised prostitution, some of which may still be hidden.

Little is known about the origins of the systems of prostitution practised in Halvagal village, but it is obvious that the inhabitants of the village continue to do so only out of dire economic need. The upper castes in this area have stripped this community of any possibility that they might break out of their historical role as prostitutes serving the more privileged groups. These men have the right to sleep with Halvagal women and girls, in the female's home, whenever they decide to pay a visit. He is under no obligation to pay them, and customarily does not. If he visits them regularly, they must even provide food and liquor.

The inhabitants of the village, who are mainly women, only

barely manage to live as daily agricultural labourers. Trapped in a system of prostitution which earns them nothing financially, these girls and women are caught up in a vicious generational cycle whereby a prostitute who has a daughter usually inducts that daughter into the system so that the mother will have somebody to take care of her when she is older. By doing this, the women themselves perpetuate the very system that oppresses them but they have no means of escape from it.

4

Tomorrow's Woman

The girlchild of today is the woman of tomorrow. The skills, ideas and energy of the girlchild are vital for full attainment of the goals of equality, development and peace. For the girlchild to develop her full potential she needs to be nurtured in an enabling environment, where her spiritual, intellectual and material needs for survival, protection and development are met and her equal rights safeguarded. If women are to be equal partners with men, in every aspect of life and development now is the time to recognise the human dignity and worth of the girlchild and to ensure to her the full enjoyment of her human rights and fundamental freedoms, including the rights assured by the Convention on the Rights of the Child, universal ratification of which is strongly urged. Yet there exists worldwide evidence that discrimination and violence against girls begin at the earliest stages and continue unabated throughout their lives. They often have less access to nutrition, physical and mental health care and education and enjoy fewer rights, opportunities and benefits of childhood and adolescence than do boys. They are often subjected to various forms of sexual and economic exploitation, paedophilia, forced prostitution and possibly the sale of their organs and tissues, violence and harmful practices such as female infanticide and prenatal sex selection, incest, female genital mutilation and early marriage, including child marriage.*

During my three decades' experience there has been an increase in meetings, conventions and discourse on prostitution of minor girls, trafficking and sexual exploitation of children, especially girlchildren. International forums, our national governments and non-governmental institutions and groups have created a voluminous discourse on the phenomenon of trafficking of young

* Para 39. The Girl child, UNICEF, India Country Office.

girls and children for prostitution. However, the imperative need today is to translate all those ideas into action.

My friend and colleague Dr. (Mrs.) Syeda S. Hameed describes one of the conferences we attended in Mumbai thus: "The five-star conference had become suffocating. The plight of the girl-child who was sold in prostitution was being discussed vigorously. One after another people got up to recount the 'situational analysis'. We had heard this refrain many times earlier. Realising that there was nothing new to learn, we got up quietly and walked out of the plush Nehru Centre into the sun.

"The city of Mumbai lay open before us. Ocean and sky were indistinguishable in their greyness. Magnolia, champa and palms were gentle reminders of the rain-forest Bombay of my childhood. I felt like a truant child who had stolen a free morning from the conference at which several hundred people were discussing threadbare every form of prostitution. But where were the women on whose account we had all gathered there? Where were these women in prostitution who had inspired people from thirteen countries to gather together for three days? Sensing my discomfort, Mohini ordered the driver, 'Chalo Falkland Avenue'. The car lunged away from the tree-lined undulations of Peddar Road and plunged into the surging humanity and car-plugged streets towards Mumbai's red-light area.

Through narrow lanes and, choked roads, on either sides of the street, in broad daylight, I saw them all. Bunches of girls were about, standing, sitting, lying. Standing in doorways, arms swinging, beckoning passers-by. Girls in skirts, saris, pants, shalwars; girls with ribbons, clips, earrings and make-up — stood and solicited. Looking at them through the rolled-up window of the car I felt voyeuristic. A small girl of nine or ten was sitting with two teenagers on the steps of a decrepit tenement. It was nothing unusual except her hair, which was too nicely curled and slicked in place. A beautiful face, an unformed body, a few years away from puberty—in retrospect prize catch for the customers at Falkland Avenue.

We slowed down before a bunch of loitering policemen. "Can you take us to a 'kotha' where we can talk to some of the women?" I asked. The men looked suspiciously at us. At a distance we spotted a policewoman on a motorcycle. That is how Nita Phadke, Subinspector, D.B. Marg Police Station, took us to Pauwala Street. The Pauwala Police Chowki was jutting out on the road. Bang in front of it was a old wreck of a building. Rows of chicken-coop rooms were visible behind the dangerously fragile balconies. As we approached the building crowd started gathering around. Nita Phadke, two or three policemen, and I were surrounded by scores of curiose people. A middle-aged woman appeared from nowhere and introduced herself as Prema Naik, social worker. Clad in a silk sari, with well-oiled hair, Prema told us that she was from Mangalore and had lived here for twenty-five years. "It is my mission to look after these girls", she said in a matter-of-fact way. We wondered whether she was a social worker, a `madam' or a `gharwali'. But were relieved that there was someone who could take us there. We wanted to meet some residents of the crumbling Simplex Mansion, an unusual name for a building on Pauwala Street.

Initially, the girls were scared of coming out. We could see them on the balconies watching us carefully. Prema sent one of the boys upstairs while we waited on the street trying to drive away the stragglers. In five minutes several men came down the dingy staircase. Seeing us these men in banians slinked into corners. To me it seemed a long wait.

The first one came down hesitantly. Black nightgown, hennaed feet, dishevelled hair, that was Parveen. Started her 'dhanda' seven years ago. She told us she was thirty-five, but looked no more than nineteen or twenty. Part of her earnings went to support her little boy who was in Calcutta with her mother. Yes she visited him once a year. Then came Baby, a tall thin girl who smiled a lot when I asked if she spoke Bangla. She was a Bihari from Calcutta. "Why did you come here?" I asked. "Swami margaya" (master died), she repeated parrot-like. She made two or three hundred rupees a day. But then there were good days and bad days. Nirmala from Nagpur made one hundred and fifty per day. But her child had to be supported in the village as also her widowed mother.

"One by one they came down to us. The story of Geeta from Tirupathi was no different. She was 'thirty-five' (looked twenty-two or so), had been in the 'dhanda' for seven years and her two sons were being brought up by her parents in the village. Yes she went to see them. On being asked how often she reptied as often as she liked. We discerned a note of defiance in the claim. My glance drifted to a figure standing silently behind in the shadows. Wrapped in a black sari, no henna, was Zarina. She did not say much. In the stark sun I saw that signs of age had appeared on her face. She said she was from Bangalore. Mohini talked to her in Kannada—very kindly, very gently. "I have a small baby with me", she said with hesitation, ' and two at home with my parents. My husband left me for another woman. I have to support my children'. 'But this child,' Mohini asked, 'whose?' What can I say Ma?' But why don't you insist on condoms?' They cost.' 'Rubbish — they are free. And even if they cost a pittance what about your health?' We saw indignation mounting. Zarina remained quiet for a moment. Then she spoke softly. 'The regulars, they don't like condoms. How can I insist? They come everyday' was her reply.

"Before my eyes a collage started forming. Zarina with a child at her breast. She servicing her regulars who insist on not using condoms. She without choices because she is getting on in years. She who cannot say no because of the two children growing up at home under the care of aging parents. Baby, Nirmala, Geeta, Parveen and Zarina. A motley of women in differing circumstances displaying their wares on the counter of lust".

"What bargaining power do these women have for health or for wages? What do they care for our five-star meetings or conferences? What do they get out of all this in concrete terms? "'Would you do anything different if we provided an alternative ?" we asked. Baby laughed, "What can I do, Ma? Only this'. Except Zarina who could read the Quran, no one could read or write. "There are no children here Madam," Prema Naik assured us. "They keep them only as long as they are breast -fed. Then they are sent away."

With tired steps and heaviness in our hearts we slowly walked towards the car where three little boys were playing 'teen patti' near an overflowing sewer. 'Destitute urchins, Madam,' Prema told us contemptuously. Her necklace was catching the sunlight, while on the balconies of the Simplex building, girls were craning their necks to scout for customers and little boys were gambling in the dirt. Certainly, a very grim past, present and future.

In 1982, Dr. I.S. Gilada, sort of pioneered public discourse and media news, in India, with the story of Tulasa, a 10-year-old girl from Nepal who was lured into the brothels in Bombay, as also the story of Begum, a 5-year-old girl who was raped by her father and subsequently sold to the brothel. The starting point of these discourses and conventions is, infinitely a horror, both personal and public.

One of the most shocking incidents that I cannot erase from my memory was during my visit to the red-light area in Ujjain. There several teenage boys surrounded me on my visit and I was so happy to note their smiling faces. However, my happiness was short-lived, when I was told that none of these children attended school but were actually engaged in the work of procuring clients for their mothers. I just stood there in disbelief not able to comprehend the fact that a child could procure customers for his own mother!

A sample of the prevailing situation can be gleaned from the following account.

The backdrop of a narrow dingy street in Gokak, Belgaum district, Karnataka. A small voice exclaims, "Ma, I want a velvet blouse. The mother, she scolded me. Father—he was always in a drunken stupor. There was hardly any food to eat. So I ran away from my house. I met this uncle at the bus stop. He promised to buy me a velvet blouse. Thereafter I don't know what happened until I found myself in a dark room in Gokak village."

The current situation is that this little fourteen-year-old child is forced to serve about twenty clients a day. She earns about ten rupees for a single day's work. Her's is the story of most of the children in prostitution. She wants to get out but is trapped. Her questions are "Where to go? How to support myself ? What about Madam's loan?" These questions remain unanswered for her.

The frightened look on the small face of the child made me wince in anguish. I want to reach out. I want to shake up the world—to eradicate the evil of poverty, to eliminate illiteracy, to provide safe and secure environment for these vulnerable children, and, ultimately, to train them in befitting vocations so that they can earn and live with dignity.

I realise that this path is ridden with difficulties. I know there is no magic wand which can be twirled to change this grim reality. I know, too, that no matter how many conferences we have, how many laws we make, the truth is that we cannot wipe off the tears from the face of every little girl who has been hurt, abused and traumatised. But there are no choices—a bold beginning has to be made.

Actually, there is no dearth of ideas and guidance for measures to effectively curb the menace. The challenge is to provide cooperation amongst all involved authorities and organizations, find the necessary funding, and effectively implement the proper legislation and measures both at national and international levels.

Minors are particularly vulnerable to physical and mental damage. That is why preventive action, like dissemination of information to children, parents and schools, and promotion of opportunities for education and employment, is especially important in combatting child trafficking.

Child trade and prostitution is a huge business, in terms of billions of US dollars in annual turnover worldwide. Criminal organizations, operating across continents, have found that trafficking in migrants is even more lucrative than drug trafficking and they often succeed in combining the two.

The term childhood generally signifies easy living, easy nutrition, love, warmth, support and an overall affectionate environment. But 15 per cent of India's two million prostitutes, believed to be children, have a different story to tell. As trafficking and prostitution among children assumes alarming proportions (nearly 200 girls and women in India are either inducted into or enter the trade everyday) we as a nation are confronted with a grim reality which is hard to ignore. No nation can afford to leave its supreme asset, its children, at the mercy and caprice of sex predators.

The term paedophilia gained currency during the 80s and 90s and is defined as sexual attraction of an adult towards a child. More often than not it is sexual desire towards pre-pubertal children. Child prostitution refers to situations in which children engage in regular sexual activity for material benefits for themselves and their families. These are sexually exploited for profit. It is an intensely depraved form of child labour. Although all prostitution is exploitative, but in the case of mature men and women there is some element of volition or consent. The corollary here is that young children do not have the capacity to give valid consent. Such a phraseology masks the truer structure of the criminal nexus of abductors, procurers, brothel managers, pimps and profiteers.

In India, despite emphasis and solemn resolves for the safeguard of a child from all sorts of abuse under the Constitution and despite the fact that India is a signatory to the UN Convention which guarantees rights of a child, the phenomenon of child-prostitution does exist in the country. This has started assuming monstrous proportions as is sometimes depicted in some of the press reports especially by the foreign media.

The problem, however, does exist. Let us first analyse the situation and circumstances how a girlchild enters the profession. To my mind, it appears, that there are four distinct ways – at times, some of these converge and overlap:

- Girls are kidnapped, induced, allured and sold (in many cases by parents themselves). Nearly 80-85 per cent of victims come into prostitution through this pathway.

- About 10 per cent are offspring of the prostitutes – unwed or wedded. In such cases even though the mothers do not like their daughters to follow them in their profession, the powerful nexus of Gharwalis (brothel keepers), pimps and pahalwans (musclemen) decide otherwise.

- Then there is caste/community specific and area-specific prostitution. Going from generation to generation, this is the type of child-prostitution which is practised in specific areas by some communities under the gaze of the family itself. Some of the known localities of operations are Mandsaur, Guna, Raisen, Bhind, Morena, Shivpuri, Gwalior in Madhya Pradesh, the region around Chakrata in Uttar Pradesh, amongst Nats and Sansis of Central India, some tribes in north-eastern states and some of the nomadic tribes following Venkatasani cult in Telangana region of Andhra Pradesh.

- And finally we have the special types — the profession with links in some of religious customs. Instances of these are the Devadasis in Karnataka, Andhra Pradesh, Orissa and Maharashtra, Bhavanis in Goa, Kudikars on West Coast, Jogins in Andhra Pradesh, Thevardiyar in Tamil Nadu, Basavis in Karnataka and Muralis, Jogateens and Aradhinis in Maharashtra.

The system of child prostitution in India is as varied as the Devadasi or the Jogini and the trafficking system, that moves young girls across the borders into South Asia's urban centres, reveals the active exploitation and the socio-economic realities that make such exploitation possible.

Mr. O' Grady, addressing the National Consultation on Child Prostitution, organised jointly by ECPAT, YMCA and UNICEF asked " .... how much is a child worth ? Even if the property is the driving force, is it worth telling your child to go into prostitution, which is almost certain death. It is not just poverty. Why does one poor family sell children to prostitution and another doesn't? These are ethical issues. It is about valuing one's child. Is it such low valuing of a child that you would let them go through the suffering, because you as parent wish to buy a TV?"

Despite legislations to curb the practice, child prostitution is on the rise in India, which has the unenviable distinction of having the largest number of child prostitutes in the world. One reason could be that no worthwhile steps are being taken to cut into the rot as police seems to have hand-in-glove relationship with the brothel-owners, keepers and pimps. New girls keep coming and most of the time the daughters of prostitutes also take to the oldest profession. Payoffs to the police by brothelkeepers are high, so even if an honest officer goes to raid a brothel, usually madams and pimps have been tipped off well in advance by other policemen.

Prosecutions are few in this particular field as prostitution is a bailable offence and often big brothels are never brought to book. A brothel owner can be sentenced to a term of nothing less than seven years for forcing children (below 16 years) in prostitution and 7-14 years for forcing minors (16-18). Further, children in brothel are masqueraded as relatives of prostitutes and due to lack of evidence the police fail to pursue the case. Even if minors are rescued, the brothelkeepers produce fake birth certificates or affidavits claiming to be the guardians/parents of the children. The juvenile courts in such situations have release the children who go back to the brothels?

While government agencies and police spend time and money looking for proof that children are being pushed into sexual slavery, thousands are having their childhood nipped in the bud everyday. Poverty has combined with an insensitive society and government apathy to push them into hopelessness.

Even though girls are neglected and wanted in certain families and communities, in prostitution-prone areas they are in good demand as customers are willing to pay even twice as much if the girls are below 18 years of age. Most of the girls in red-light areas are pushed into the trade at a very tender age. While earlier this tender age was 12-13 years, today it has decreased to 8-10 years. A survey in Bihar revealed that roadside dhabas in the Aurangabad and Sasaram districts provide girls to the truck drivers who fall in the age group of 6-18 years.

A study conducted by the National Commission for Women showed that 60 per cent of the prostitutes in red-light area of G.B. Road, Delhi are child prostitutes. Further, approximately, 4.25 per cent between the age group of 8-15 are brought from Bangladesh and Nepal, and they form an important component of child prostitutes in Delhi.

According to psychiatrists, the customers of the child prostitutes are adults who suffer from poor self-image and are emotionally deprived. Moreover, sex with a child gives many aging men a temporary sense of being youthful. Another reason is the widespread myth that sex with a virgin can cure impotency and sexually transmitted diseases.

Most of the child prostitutes do not carry out the profession by themselves. It is patronized by four categories of people such as brothelkeeper, pimp, procurer and customer. The child prostitutes are mostly slaved, battered and exploited and misused by their "professional boss" for making money through easy means. These children are often forced to grow in the midst of the worst conditions of life.

Once she enters the profession she has no other way out of it. She is inescapably caught in the trap even if she cries, pleads and rebels. If she refuses she is subject to inhuman conditions, she is held captive in a little dingy room which has no ventilation. She is tortured and threatened by various means mercilessly. Her body, mind and soul are brutally raped repeatedly. At times she is forced to entertain as many as 20 customers each night. Sometimes these hapless victims are turned into drug addicts and alcoholics so that they succumb to the greed and lust of perverted men. Then, is it any surprise that immediately after induction into the trade these young girls of average 13-14 years, develop a number of dreadful diseases? Then later they have children who cannot be looked after when they are young, while usually it is these very children who grow up to become perpetuators of this profession!

If miraculously, the vicious circle is broken, and the girl manages to escape, she finds that there are very few options left for her since firstly, her family refuses to accept her back into the family fold; secondly, they are illiterate without any skill and lastly she carries the stigma of being a prostitute. If at all, she manages to survive, somehow in the society such as ours, which has set and adopted different standards for man and woman does not allow her to live in peace. The plight of such girls can be highlighted by my experience. About 16 years ago, when I was the Chairperson of the War Widows Association, I got a call from a hospital in Delhi asking me if I could come and help a young, unaccompanied 15-16-year-old girl from G.B. Road, who had just delivered a stillborn child. Apparently, the girl was weeping hysterically and speaking Kannada which nobody but the attending doctor understood.

I rushed there as soon as I could, and found the girl sobbing repeatedly that she had been kidnapped from her home in Karnataka and sold into a brothel in Delhi. The girl said if she went back home, nobody will accept her and she did not wish to go back to the brothel either . She pleaded with the doctors that as her child was already dead, that they may declare her dead as well so that "they" — the brothelkeeper might not seek her later.

I took the girl home and after a few days enrolled her in a training programme that helped her get a job with a family I knew. She stayed with them for nearly four years until one morning a samosa vendor on the road was called into the house for some purchases. He caught sight of this girl and immediately burst out "*Arrey*, you are here; everybody at G.B. Road thought you were dead for these last four years..." She was struck with terror and subsequently I had to shift her.

This is how all "rescue" and "rehabilitation" goes down the drain for a girl when an ordinary samosawalla (a man) could walk in and shatter it all in a second.

The 'Buds' of the Prostitute

Going through the streets of Kamatipura, Sonagachi, Madurai, Calicut, Lucknow, Muzzafarpur, one cannot but notice the hordes of children on the streets. There were babies being breast-fed, babies being bathed, children playing hopscotch on the streets, children wailing for attention, all of them yearning for love, attention and care.

For days together after these visits I could not sleep thinking about these little buds in the jungle of thorns. The question foremost in my mind was why were these women in prostitution producing so many children? I looked around for answers and everywhere throughout the length and breadth of the country the women in prostitution told me that these little buds were their future security.

The women in prostitution want to have children because they perceive a child as something of their own and the only link with life on whom they could shower true love and maintain trusting relationship in their harsh and doomed existence. The desire to have a child can be further explained in the words of a prostitute mother as – "men may come and go after using us, but it is my child who will be my support. I shall therefore not mind doing anything for the upbringing of my child even if it means to stay away from him or her for his or her betterment".

The children of prostitutes are vulnerable to the ways of the trade, right from birth. These children, from the very beginning of their lives are stamped with the stigma of being illegitimate. Few of these children have fathers. Either the father has abandoned the family or the children are born to the mothers by customers. However, the illegitimate status is reminded to these children by the people around as well by the society in more than one way. Education, health programmes or any other facility is not provided to them.

In the absence of a father, the mother becomes the most important person in the child's life. In red-light areas, there is no family or healthy social environment. Hence, the physical and psychological well-being of a child connected to family environment is also denied to these children. In such a situation if the child looks upon society for a helping hand that is refused to him, instead, numerous denigrating remarks are showered upon him, resulting in the widening of the gap between these children and society and, consequently, the child's life is affected.

Ultimately, these children grow up in the environment which exposes them to the scum of society like pimps, brothelkeepers, the hafta receiving police, the procurer, bootleggers, alcoholics, drug-peddlers and addicts, etc.

The mothers usually have no time to devote for their children. When she gets up late in the mornings, maybe later, the children are already awake for several hours and are waiting since her to give them something to eat. Since she had been practising the trade till the wee hours of the morning and as she would usually be tired, and may be, she might have a hangover too if she had consumed excessive liquor the previous night.

Meanwhile, the children are playing outside the house, i.e. on the streets, at garbage dumps and on the beach. Sometimes, when the mother keeps on sleeping, the older children may themselves prepare tea and eat the leftovers. At times, when there is nothing in the house the children go out begging for food in the vicinity, at bars or in the restaurants. Often mothers encourage children to go for begging.

Among the children, there are several "gangs" whose members stick together and are involved in activities such as begging, bootlegging, gambling and sleeping together at night. When the mother gets up she is busy with domestic work and is often assisted by her children. She is also busy with preparing herself for another day in the trade. As the mothers are busy with the trade, children are again left on their own. In absence of any constructive activity, the most common way for them to spend time is to loiter around in the vicinity in the streets of the red-light area.

Here, they mix with people such as criminals and drug dealers. These people may ask the children to run errands for them which may involve handing over drugs also and little girls among them are subjected to eve-teasing and sexual abuse too. In this way, the children are gradually drawn into criminal activities.

As the mothers do not have any place of their own, the children sleep on the pavements. At times quarrels or fights occur, sleeping outside in cold may result in these children developing cold, pneumonia and other diseases. Again, sleeping outside alone or with other children is also a risky activity as they are exposed to other men in the area, who sometimes take advantage of the situation and molest the child. When the child sleeps inside it cannot avoid watching and hearing what is going on between their mother and the customer. These scenes can be rough and terrifying for a child to assuemilate. Exposures to these kind of scenes leads to bad sleep, nightmares and hatred for men, whom the child sees as exploiters of its mothers. The child also develops a sense of loneliness as it rarely gets an opportunity to sleep next to his mother and feel her love and protection.

In the case of tiny-tots, children are put to sleep below the bed which are used by women for their business. These infants are treated with contempt by the brothelkeepers on the grounds that they take too much of their mother's time. Very often mothers drug them to put them off to sleep, which on one hand prevents them from becoming a nuisance for the mothers and on the other hand slowly results in damage to their mental and physical states.

The children also witness their mothers being ill-treated by the brothelkeepers which at times reaches the height of cruelty. Often, slightly older children are made to clean and settle the rooms for business purposes at their mother's behest, while they dress up. Though certain mothers show their desire to educate their children and at times even manage to send them to school but the stigma of being "children of prostitute" never let them rest in peace whether at school or in college or even in jobs. One such girl who managed to enter college for graduation had ultimately to drop out because her friends had become aware of her background. Then, in another instance, in Ujjain, a girl had to lose a job in All India Radio which she had got on basis of merit just because she had given her correct address, that of the infamous red-light area of the city.

Hence, these children suffer from strange psychological strains and emotional complexities. This lead to their becoming rebellious, abusive, violent and consequently they develop aggressiveness and hatred towards one and all and show a general pessimistic attitude towards life.

The children have difficulties in developing a healthy identity. The girl children are always in touch with their mothers and brothel madams who set a distorted picture as a role model. She observes her mother mostly in bad situations, such as drinking, liquor and using foul and abusive language, taking drugs, and of course being in the sex trade. For boys, they observe their role model in customers, pimps and criminals who can hardly be seen as positive role models. In the absence of a father, and with a busy mother there is no one to morally guide the child. They develop their own moral codes by absorbing the surrounding environment among the pimps, brothel madam, customers and other shady figures. Owing to lack of education, employment and any constructive activity, the children have little choice and gradually they get dragged into prostitution and various other criminal activities.

There are many dimensions to the problem of child prostitution. Power relationships are of utmost importance. The powerful haves, those who are better armed and more equipped with technology and state-of-the art communication systems, always have their way in the world. The perenially victimised are the have-nots, the powerless. In terms of these value systems those who are the poorest, most helpless and at the bottom of the heap are but the children! Paedophilia and child prostitution zeroes in on the issue of exploitation in relationships of unequal power. First there is the child himself or herself—too young to be aware of the relationship that is struck with the client. Secondly there is class exploitation—the children are recruited from economically depressed families who have no means of fighting the excesses of paedophiles. In capitalistic societies there is a massive commodification of sex. Here the child is reduced to a commodity to be exchanged for a sum of money.

However, an interesting development is underway in the red-light areas of the megapolises of our country. The women already inducted into the profession in these areas realise that it is the only livelihood they are going to be allowed by society. But they also want to revolt against the monetary exploitation. As a result they no lenger consider it profitable to function as brothel inmates since the money goes to the brothelkeepers. So many of them have started functioning as call girls. While this option is available to women in towns and cities, in rural areas, the women in prostitution are still largely from communities that have been traditionally engaged in entertainment.

The mental trauma and agony of prostituted children is best described by Renee Bridet, an eminent French jurist as "even if they are alive, they are dying within". The Allahabad High Court judgement on the Uttarakhand agitation, while determining the quantum of compensation to rape victims, treated rape as a crime equivalent to murder, considering the psychological onslaught.

5

Trafficking : The Modern Slavery

"Trafficking is the contemporary form of ancient slavery. Its bonds are not shackles of iron but poverty."

– Prof. Ishrat Shamim, President,
Centre for Women and Children Studies

Trafficking for Prostitution and Slave-like Work in Asia
Inputs on Trafficking in Women and Girls

Sending Countries

Bangladesh
Myanmar
Korea
Laos
Nepal
Philippines
Sri Lanka
Thailand
Vietnam

Receiving Countries

Hong Kong
India
Japan
Combodia
Malaysia
Middle East
Pakistan
Taiwan

Means of Procurement

- Kidnapping/abduction
- Promises of better jobs
- Procuring through marriage/ fake marriages
- Selling of girls by parents/ husbands
- Deceiving women and girls for legal or illegal migration
- Rape or sexually abusing women and girls

Type of Work

- Prostitution
- Mail-order bride
- Domestic work
- Work in sex tourism industry
- Factory work
- Cabaret dancers
- Barmaids
- Bonded labour

Consequences on Women and Girls

- Psychological trauma
- Mental abnormality
- Unwanted pregnancy
- Drug addiction
- Sexually Transmitted Diseases
- HIV/AIDS
- Stigmatization as social outcasts

Trafficking is a term that subtly allows commodification, an act which we seemingly protest against especially when directed towards women.

Besides this Janusian political product, the compact term conceals the diversity of acts involved, from seduction, allurement, abduction, confinement, threats and actual violence (called "breaking down" by the members of the inner circle).

Trafficking mainly refers to transportation of girls/women by road/rail or other means of transport for monetary consideration of the persons engaged in trafficking. The purpose of trafficking may be twofold: (a) flesh trade, and (b) marriage. Whatever may be the aim, it necessarily involves:

(a) presence of procurers and potential buyers of girls/women who are motivated by economic gain;
(b) non-involvement of the victims (girls/women) in the whole exercise ; and
(c) induction of women, in many cases, into flesh trade.

Trafficking occurs throughout the world in different forms but trafficking of women and children is a serious and brutal reality of the Asian region. Trafficking includes illegal adoption, thefts of body parts, debt bondage of workers and commercial sexual exploitation of children which is a problem most pernicious in nature.

Trafficking is defined as the illegal moving and selling of human beings across and within the countries and continents in exchange for monetary and/or other compensation. It has long been outlawed by national legislation and international human rights treaties but despite this, the trafficking of women and children remains a multibillion dollar industry ranked by many governments as the third most serious illegal trade after drugs and armaments. This form of violence on children is flourishing like a major industry/business controlled by well organized international crime syndicates. Since it is lucrative, innumerable strong criminal networks are very actively involved in the trafficking of children from one state to another and from one country to another contributing to the rapid growth of this form of violence on both female/male children / adolescent from a very tender age. They are bartered at prices that vary depending on their age, beauty and virginity, and exploited under conditions that amount to modern form of slavery. Women and girls who have been trafficked can rarely escape or negotiate the conditions of their employment. Many police officers and other local government officials facilitate and profit from the trade in women and girls. For a price, they ignore the crimes that occur in their jurisdictions, protect the traffickers, brothel-owners, pimps, clients and buyers from arrest, and serve as enforcers, drivers and recruiters. If a child or a woman is taken across national borders, immigration officials frequently aid and abet their passage.

Although traffic in women and girl possesses distinct characteristics in each country or region where it occurs, certain patterns have emerged that cut across geographical boundaries. In a typical situation, a woman or girl is first recruited by an agent with promises of good job in another country or province. For instance, Bangladeshi and Nepali women and girls are promised the opportunity to escape poverty at home to the relative prosperity of Pakistan and India, respectively. Women and girls have also been abducted outright, as some testimonies from Bangladesh or Nepal indicate.

During my visit to Bangladesh, Salma Ali of the Women's Lawyers' Association took me to a red-light area and the visit to the brothel showed the sordid conditions in which thousands of young girls were living. There were narrow dingy lanes, where they were bathing, cooking, washing clothes and soliciting customers. Each cabin had a small curtain and little girls were looking out curiously at me from behind the curtains. Suddenly a young girl pulled the pallu of my saree and very softly, with tears rolling down her big eyes, implored me to take her away. I looked around and softly urged Salma to somehow or the other smuggle out that little girl. Salma at once took the girl between us both and on the pretense of going to the bathroom, we slowly steered our way to the car which was standing on the main road. We bundled the little girl on the floor of the car and told the driver to drive quickly. Looking out of the screen Salma and myself found the pimps chasing and screaming at us. There was a heavy traffic jam on the road and very soon the pimps caught up with us and were banging on the glass of the car. Fortunately Salma had a mobile phone and she called up the nearest police station to rescue us from the pimps. Our hearts were pounding and the journey back to the Women's Lawyers' Association was one of intense fright and tension. If rescuing can be that difficult how are we going to face the challenges? The girl told us her story of how she was lured into the brothel on the pretext of getting a job. Yet another mode of recruitment is through false marriage offers, with the bride later being sold off to a brothel.

Once recruited or abducted, virtually all women and girls trafficked are forced into prostitution and are controlled through debt bondage. The initial debt is usually a payment to the women's family at the time of recruitment, which she must repay, with interest, by working in a brothel. This "debt" mounts as the brothel-owners add on the cost of food, clothes, medicine and other expenses. Escape is virtually impossible without repaying the "debt", since leaving the brothel puts the woman at the risk of punishment by the brothel-owner, his employees or the police, retribution against her parents and other relatives for defaulting on her debt, and/or arrest as an illegal immigrant. The women trafficked or sold into forced marriage are also held captive through financial obligations. The distance from home, lack of familiarity with the local language or dialect and inability to find local support networks further reinforce the women's and girl's dependence on the brothel-owners, pimps or "husbands".

The sun was setting over the Hubli river when Jyotsna, Indrani and myself were listening to the music of small voices in a dingy makeshift creche for children at Sonagachi. Suddenly, a beautiful 18- year-old girl came running into the classroom sat down at my feet and holding on to them softly said, "Please take me away in your car. I am a Christian girl, I have passed Xth class and I want to go back to Darjeeling". She said that she was sold for Rs. 20,000/-, that I should arrange for that sum to be returned to the Madam and take her away. Jyotsna and myself looked at each other not knowing what to do? I had a sudden revulsion for myself, while I was listening to her. Why did I come to Sonagachi, if I can't even release one person from bondage? There are thousands of Marys who want to get out. What legal mechanisms can we frame to release them from bondage?

Victims of forced prostitution in particular are exposed to health risks, especially sexually transmitted diseases (STDs), because they are not allowed to negotiate the terms of sex. Aside from risk of infection through sexual intercourse with many clients, the growing popularity of contraceptive injections in brothels also contributes to the spread of disease, since brothel owners often use the same and possibly contaminated needle several times. For women who develop AIDS, forced prostitution is ultimately fatal. Other women have become infertile due to STDs and, thus, do not remain eligible for marriage in cultures where the primary purpose of marriage is procreation. Shunned by their own families and communities, many of these women must return to prostitution in order to support themselves.

Because prostitution is illegal in most countries and prostitutes are scorned upon in virtually all, victims of forced prostitution face legal and moral isolation. Out of fear of social ostracism, women are reluctant to speak about their experiences of abuse and thus to warn others who might also be vulnerable. This isolation infringes on their liberties and human rights are violated.

International attempts to eradicate trafficking in women were made as early as 1904 when the International Agreement for the Suppression of the White Slave Trade (as trafficking in women was then called) was signed in Paris. The agreement sought to provide for the tradition of coercive procurement of women and any procurement and transportation of girls from one country to another for immoral purposes. Further, efforts can be found in the International Convention for the Suppression of White Slave Traffic in 1910, the Convention for the Suppression of the Traffic in Women and Children, 1921 and the Convention for the Suppression of the Traffic in Women of Full Age, 1933. The instruments were consolidated in 1949. Thus, the modern standards on the elimination of trafficking in women, are based on the 1949 Convention for the Suppression of the Traffic in Persons and of the Exploitation of Prostitution of Others. (*see AnnexureII*). In the nearly fifty years, since, the adoption of the 1949 International Convention on the Trafficking in Persons, a number of international legal instruments have been developed that deal at least in part, with the trafficking in women. However, despite the growth of instruments in this area, it cannot yet be said that an international legal regime exists that successfully governs this complex problem.

Trafficking in persons has long been recognized as a contemporary form of slavery. In an effort to provide adequate protection to victims of this practice, early conventions against slavery have been supplemented by international agreements concerning trafficking, such as the 1949 Convention on Trafficking in Persons. Yet, the contemporary face of slavery has changed immeasurably ever since 1949. Unfortunately, developments in methods of detection and prevention have not kept pace with the creation of new forms of trafficking.

As the phenomenon of trafficking in women and children becomes increasingly global and modern, new legal approaches are emerging to combat the problem. (*see Annexure I*) A lot more work needs to be done at the level of the international standard to ensure the basic rights of the summary deportation of trafficked persons and the lack of support services for them. This work is critical to shift the focus from the prosecution of the traffickers to the needs of victims, and to make it easier for victims to seek help and speak out about their situations.

International customary law also condemns slavery and slave-like practices (inherent in traffic in women) so that those countries which have not ratified the instruments are under international obligation to take measures for the eradication of traffic in women and children. Moreover, anti-slavery conventions also apply to traffic in women.

States have, in recent pronouncements, renewed their commitment to the eradication of traffic in women. The 1993 World Conference on Human Rights reaffirmed that the human rights of women and of the girl child are an inalienable, integral and indivisible part of universal human rights. The Conference Declaration also states that: "Gender-based violence and all forms of sexual harassment and exploitation, including those resulting from cultural prejudice and international trafficking, are incompatible with the dignity and worth of the human person, and must be eliminated."

The Declaration on the Elimination of Violence against Women unanimously adopted by the United Nations General Assembly in 1993 confirms that traffic in women is a form of violence against women, which must be eliminated. Under Article 4(c) and (e) States are called upon to exercise due diligence to prevent, investigate and, in accordance with national legislation, punish acts of violence against women, whether those acts are perpetrated by the State or by private individuals and to consider the possibility of developing national plans of action to promote the protection of women against any form of violence, or to include provisions for this purpose in plans already existing, taking into account, as appropriate, such cooperation as can be provided by non-governmental organizations, particularly those concerned with this subject.

Strategic Objective D-3 of the Beijing Declaration and Platform for Action adopted at the Fourth World Conference on Women at Beijing in 1995, addressed the elimination of trafficking in women and assistance to victims of forced prostitution and trafficking. It calls upon countries of origin, transit and destination to:

(a) Consider the ratification and enforcement of international conventions on trafficking in persons and on slavery;
(b) Take appropriate measures to address the root factors, including external factors that encourage trafficking in

women and girls for prostitution and other forms of commercialized sex, forced marriages, and forced labour in order to eliminate trafficking in women, including by strengthening existing legislation with a view to providing better protection of the rights of women and girls and to punishing the perpetrators, through both criminal and civil measures;

(c) Step up cooperation and concerted action by all relevant law enforcement authorities and institutions with a view to dismantling national, regional and international networks of trafficking;

(d) The first ever World Congress against Commercial Sexual Exploitation of Children was organized by End Child Prostitution in Asian Tourism (ECPAT) and UNICEF. Hosted by the Swedish Government it was held in Stockholm in August, 1996. The meeting aimed to bring together a mixture of NGOs, governments, the police and the children concerned to agree on an Agenda for Action. This Agenda was signed by representatives of all the 119 governments who attended the Congress including India.

The governments committed themselves to combatting the commercial sexual exploitation of children (CSEC) at a number of levels. At the local level, they agreed to the creation of national agendas for action with specific and achievable goals by the year 2000, and to the formation of national databases of vulnerable children and their exploiters. The Agenda also contains an appeal for greater interaction between governments an appeal for greater interaction between governments and NGOs in the planning, implementation and evaluation of projects aimed at countering CSEC. It advocates greater cooperation levels at regional, international and non-governmental organizations identified as having vital roles in the elimination of CSEC and recommends they take guidance from the Agenda in their activities. Moreover, it stresses the need for the full implementation of the Convention on the Rights of the Child.

In the Fifty-first Session of the United Nations General Assembly held in New York on 14th November, 1996, 43 countries adopted a resolution on the traffic in women and girls. In the said resolution, governments are called upon to implement the Platform for Action of the Fourth World Conference on Women. It also encourages cooperation and concerted action by law-enforcing authorities and institution so as to dismantle national, regional and international networks in trafficking. Governments are also asked to criminalize trafficking in women and girls in all its forms and to condemn and penalize all those offenders involved, including intermediaries, regardless of the place where the offences are committed, while ensuring that victims of trafficking are not penalized; and to penalize persons in authority found guilty of sexually assaulting victims of trafficking in their custody. — *Coalition Asia-Pacific Report.*

During the 53rd session of the Commission on Human Rights held in Geneva from March 10th to April 17th, 1997, many women activists gathered and lobbied for the integration of gender perspective into UN human rights mechanisms. The report of the Special Rapporteur, Ms. Radhika Coomaraswamy covered the issue of rape and sexual violence against women including sexual harassment and trafficking in women and forced prostitution. In her recommendation on trafficking in women, she urged the international community to begin a dialogue towards adoption of new international standards with regard to trafficking and prostitution. Such standards, she further suggested, "should be developed along with international mechanisms to ensure reporting and monitoring of State activities."

According to ECPAT (End Child Prostitution in Asian Tourism, Child Pornography and Trafficking of Children for Sexual Purposes), a Thailand-based international NGO, children have been smuggled from Asia to Europe using forged passports and false evidence marriage or adoption. According to the same source, the Japanese mafia is involved in child trafficking in Thailand.

It seems that regardless of the continent, wherever child traffickers see potential for their business, their recruiting methods follow a similar pattern. Recruiters hit impoverished rural areas in the poorest countries. They make friends with the parents or the children themselves, give false promises of jobs and education for the kids in the cities, and pay money to the parents. Worse, sometimes the parents even know what is waiting for their children, yet they take the money and let them go.

The growing number of stories about child trafficking — a particularly heinous form of irregular migration and abuse of human rights—has contributed to alerting governments and prompting them to action. As with other forms of trafficking, a wide variety of measures need to be taken to increase preventive action, punish the criminals and help the victims. As children are especially vulnerable to the damages caused by sexual exploitation, responses that are addressed to the supply side, aiming to prevent trafficking, seek particular importance. Awareness raising, dissemination of information to all relevant groups, legislation to protect the victims while strongly punishing traffickers and abusers also extra-territorially, are called for, as well as measures to promote education and employment.

Even a cursory look at the international response and mechanisms for the eradication of traffic in women confirms the inadequacy of the standards and mechanisms for monitoring implementations. It also indicates an underlying weakness in understanding trafficking as a concept divorced from moral connotations against prostitution. There is need for work at a conceptual level and aided with empirical research, taking into account the views of women, so that developments of law at the international level respond to the reality.

Tourism

Tourism is now an organised, profit-making and expanding industry. In 1951, the year accepted as the beginning of organised tourism in India, total tourist arrivals in India was just 16,829 which has grown to 2.12 million in 1995. At present tourism is India's second largest net foreign exchange earner after readymade garments export. During the Eighth Plan period, foreign exchange earnings through tourism per year grew from Rs. 2613 crores in 1990-91 to Rs. 6509 crores in 1993-94. Total foreign exchange earnings during the plan period was Rs. 27,440 crores, whereas the Eighth Plan allocation for tourism was a measly Rs. 240 crores only.

Investigations revealed that the rate of increase of child prostitutes is in direct proportion to the growth of tourism. Tourists (especially men) come from different places of the world for cheap and easy sexual gratification in the developing countries.

India has become a safe passage for those who are involved in trafficking of minors and young women for prostitution, cheap labour and beggary. West Bengal is one of the main places through which girls are trafficked from Nepal and Bangladesh. Currently Tripura is also coming up fast in this network. Bihar and U.P. were always there and jointly these States have taken the responsibility of receiving and sending child prostitutes.

The Traffickers

The traffickers are most typically men in their twenties or thirties or women in their thirties and forties who have travelled the route to the city several times and know the hotels to stay in and the brokers to contact. They frequently work in groups of two or more. Male and female traffickers are sometimes referred to as *dalals* and *dalalis* (commission agents), who are either employed by a brothel-owner directly or operate independently. Professional agents who recruit for the bigger brothels reportedly may be paid up to Rs.10,000 per girl. But most traffickers are small-time, local recruiters who earn considerably less. In either case, to stay in business they need the patronage of local bosses and the protection afforded by bribes to the police.

Female traffickers are referred to as didi. They are themselves prostitutes now working at managerial level, may be brothel-keepers or owners also. They return to their native places or in some poverty-stricken remote villages with lot of money and jewellery to show off and attract young girls. For instance, in Nepal, the peak trafficking months in Nuwakot and Sindhupalchowk are between June and late August or early September when the didis return to the villages to participate in local festivals and to recruit girls to bring back to the cities. These months precede the harvest, when poverty is felt most acutely, making it easy to recruit. These women are exceptionally well placed to identify trafficking victims because they already know the local girls and their families.

At times, family members—uncles, cousins, stepfathers, brother-in-laws and even husbands also act as trafficking agents. According to a report from Nepal, girls are recruited in a number of ways. Village girls and their families are often deceived by smartly dressed young men who arrive in the village claiming to have come from Kathmandu and offering marriage and all the comforts of modern urban life. They go through a local ceremony and leave the village never to be seen again. The girls end up in Indian brothels. Sometimes older men promise the girls employment in the city. Another avenue is through distant relatives or friends in another village, who instead abduct the girl and send her to India. Sometimes a trusted individual abducts the girl on the pretext of educating her in India.

These local agents buy girls from their families for a meagre sum, tempt them with promises of future earnings, and take them to the Indian border where they are sold to a broker for a higher amount. These middlemen then sell them to brothel owners in Mumbai and elsewhere for still higher price depending on the girl's age, beauty and virginity. This purchase price, plus interest (almost 10% of the total) becomes the "debt" that the women are told to pay off through prostitution. Because only the brothel-owner and not the girls have any idea how much they owe or the terms for repayment, they often "pay back" indefinitely.

Trafficking in women and children is one serious and brutal reality of life in Asia. It is of grave concern amongst human rights and women's organisation working in the region which have taken up cudgels to remove this malaise afflicting the society.

Some Modes of Trafficking

Trafficking takes a number of form like : trafficking of women and children for prostitution; trafficking of little boys as jockeys for camel racing; trafficking of babies and young children through adoption for treacherous purposes like begging, stealing, etc; trafficking of women as "mail order" brides; trafficking of women and children for their organs; trafficking of young children for pornography and trafficking of children for cheap bonded labour.

India acts both as "receiving" and "sending" country. "Receiving" because girls are trafficked in Indian region from neighbouring countries of Bangladesh, Nepal, Pakistan and Sri Lanka. India is a "sending" country as the girls are trafficked from India to Pakistan, Gulf countries, and other Western countries. Sometimes girls are trafficked through Indian cities. Traffickers pick up girls from Bangladesh and to reach Pakistan they travel through India.

Inter and Intra-State Trafficking

It is not always that other countries are involved but inter-state trafficking is very much prevalent in India. A simple survey in any one of the major metropolitan cities like Delhi or Mumbai will reveal this factor. By categorizing the girls according to their place of origin this can be easily demonstrated. A survey done by the National Commission for Women revealed that in Delhi's famous red-light area, girls came from Andhra Pradesh , Bihar, Karnataka, Madhya Pradesh, Maharashtra, Rajasthan, Tamil Nadu and Uttar Pradesh besides Bangladesh and Nepal. Similarly, for Mumbai's brothels; girls are recruited from Andhra Pradesh, Karnataka, Kerala, Tamil Nadu, Uttar Pradesh, West Bengal, Delhi, Goa and Nepal.

Besides Delhi and Mumbai, girls from West Bengal are taken to Uttar Pradesh, Maharashtra, Rajasthan right up to Jammu and Kashmir and also to the Gulf countries, Pakistan and other foreign countries.

Further, girls from tribal communities where prostitution is a traditional practice, are regularly transported to major cities. For instance, Bedia girls can be found in Nagpur, Indore, Raipur, Delhi, Calcutta and Mumbai, as these girls are constantly under the control of men of their tribe. At times, these men pass these girls into the hands of traffickers who ship them to Gulf countries. Bedias are known for their ability to develop, maintain and control a trafficking route that extends from Agra in Uttar Pradesh to Morena in Madhya Pradesh and thence to numerous major cities.

Similarly, girls who have already been inducted into the Devadasi system and though their initiation ceremony had taken place in village these girls practise the trade in urban brothels. A survey reports reveals that in Mumbai, a significant percentages of girl child prostitute belong to this category (about 15-20 per cent); in urban centres on the border of Maharashtra and Karnataka they constitute 8 per cent of the total population while in Pune about 50 per cent of child prostitutes are Devadasis.

Devadasi trafficking network is very well established. The traffickers concerned are well informed on the ins and outs of the Devadasi system, and they target only those locals of intense dedication activity. Sometimes, the traffickers connect with the girl's parents even before the initiation ceremony and offer to pay for it and the girls are then shunted off to an urban brothel after which receive their commission. Other Devadasis must undergo a tour of their region's trafficking system: they are first brought to a brothel in a smaller urban area such as Nipani, a tobacco-trading centre in Maharashtra. One trafficker having received his payment, might leave a Devadasi in such a town. Since it is also a most frequent targets of traffickers, who come from major urban areas like Mumbai, the girl might ultimately be shifted to a larger city after a journey profiting numerous individuals and involving several States. (*UNICEF report,1996*)

Indo-Nepal Trafficking

Nepal is one of the poorest countries in the world with per capita income of about US $ 210. About 90 per cent of its twenty million people live in the rural areas and depend on subsistence agriculture. Life expectancy at birth is 55 years. Nepal is one of the only three countries in the world where the life expectancy at birth for females is 53.52 years as compared to 54.88 years for males and the infant mortality rate is 92 per 1,000. Sixty per cent of the population is illiterate. Health and education indicators for women are particularly discouraging. Female literacy is very low at about 25 per cent.

The social status of Nepalese women is very low. Even from birth the girl child is discriminated against. The main reason for the discrimination is age-old patriarchal social values and norms, which give very high importance to the son. The birth of a baby boy is welcomed by celebrating and rejoicing. There is a saying "let it be late, but let it be a son" which sufficiently reveals the psyche of the Nepalese traditional society. The son symbolizes success. Sons and not daughters are viewed as guardians of the old parents and perpetuators of the family tree, even by women. Daughters are described as "someone else's property". This is another reflection of the traditional psyche. Nepal reportedly has one of the highest indices of son preference in the world. Sons are desired because they represent insurance for old age and inheritors of family property. Daughters do not have the rights of inheritance of family property. In Nepalese society it is only the sons who have the rights and duty to perform the last rites of the parents. Many parents claim that they have son-preference basically for this reason.

Girl trafficking is one of the major forms of sexual exploitation in Nepal. Every year thousands of Nepali girls born in poverty and hardship end up in prostitution. An estimated 200,000 Nepali girls, among which 30 per cent are minors, work as prostitutes in India and other parts of the world.

It is difficult to say what are the origins of trafficking in girls in Nepal. Its different forms seem to have existed for the last several decades. Some 150 years ago a law was promulgated to ban the sale of girls as slaves, a practice that was prevalent in some communities. This was long before the abolition of slavery in Nepal. During the last fifty years, trafficking of Nepalese girls and women has increased very rapidly. For centuries Nepalese hill people have been migrating seasonally or permanently to populated areas in access of its carrying capacity. In the absence of farming activities or any other form of employment in the community, youths have been leaving home in search of livelihood. When the British started recruiting the young Nepalese into their army over a century ago, this tradition became glamorous. Ex-British Army men came back with enviable incomes and status. In addition to the British, India and some other countries have continued the practice of recruiting Nepalese youngmen into their army and police force. There is a theory that the young mountain-men's tradition of leaving home for jobs has had strong influence on young girls. It is a historical fact that the young and beautiful mountain girls were "offered" to the palaces where they served as maids, concubines, dancers or singers. Some palaces had thousands of such girls and some have even become "queens".

In 1951, when the Rana rule was over and Nepal became a democratic country, the young mountain girls, instead of the Rana palaces, found their place in the brothels of India. With time, this practice became more lucrative and grew to the proportion that exists today. It is believed that Nepalese girls are globally involved in the sex trade. The magnitude of this problem is enormous. Its origin and ramifications are complex. Girls trafficked to India received much attention in the Press since *The Times of India* published an article in January, 1989 saying that, according to Indian Health Organization there were approximately 100,000 Nepali girls working in the brothels of India. There is enough evidence to show that annually thousands of girls are trafficked to India, including several thousnd Nepali girls who are working in the Indian sex industry*.

Nepal is the most significant identifiable source of child prostitutes for Indian brothels. More than a million Nepalese girls are working in Indian brothels and this number is tremendously increasing each year. The average age of Nepali girls entering Indian brothels is 10-14 years. It is most unlikely that this journey is undertaken by these young girls alone. Most of the Nepali girls belong to the ethnic minority groups such as the Tamong, Gurung, Magar and Sherpa while some belong to tribal groups -- Kabre, Rasua and Dhading. The rest belong to the Hindu community. The routes followed by traffickers is generally as follows : Village — Kathmandu — Kakarvitta — Siliguri — Calcutta; village — Jagbarri — Sitamarihi — Mumbai; Nuwakot — Kathmandu — Jogbani — Patna — Delhi — Dholpur — Alwar — Mumbai Nuwakot — Kathmandu — Sonauli — Gorakhpur — Delhi — Dharpur — Alwar — Mumbai.

Economic stress and the oppression of the Nepalese girlchild, combined with the immense profits that accrue to the successful traffickers of Nepalese girls, all contribute to the rapidity of the flow of Nepalese girls to India. Nepali girls who are fair skinned,

---

Acknowledgement : Sexual Exploitation of Nepalese Girls by Mrs. Durga Ghimire, President ABC, Nepal.

delicate of features and completely helpless in the foreign country of India are the most demanded category of prostitutes in the Indian and the Gulf brothels. Traffickers are, of course, well aware of the huge profits that Nepalese girls can bring to them, so they are particularly eager to lure these girls from their homes.

However, the girls who are moved across the border either by the traffickers or by their own family members or even by their own desire, work in this profession for some time, say ten years, and return back to their community. If the girl returns with lot of money she is very well accepted and at times she may even marry and spend a decent life. Others, not so lucky ones who develop STDs or AIDS may also come back but spend their rest of life in some sanatorium.

Indo-Bangladesh Trafficking

Bangladesh is a developing country with a poor economic background. Nearly eighty-five per cent of the population has to face economic hardships. As a result, poor and disadvantaged women and children are often trafficked to India, Pakistan, and the Middle East. The major route used for this purpose covers sky, land and waterways. The victims are either abducted or enticed away with promises of a better life. Often, they are bluffed with fake marriages. The truth is that the poor and disadvantaged women of Bangladesh often fall into the trap of underworld mafia.

Bangladesh is surrounded by India on three sides – in the north, east and west. In the south, there is the Bay of Bengal. Mostly, the women are taken out of country through land routes, along the border areas of Bangladesh and India. Calcutta is the important transit point for the traffickers for Mumbai and to Pakistan. The border areas generally used are Jessore, Satkhira, Rajshahi, Meherpur, Dinajpur and Thakurgaon. The collection points of women are usually far from the border points. Bangladeshi women are sold as bonded labour and for prostitution and children are sold for prostitution, organ trade and for camel race in the Middle East.

(* Source: Bangladesh National Women's Lawyers' Association)

The major route followed for trafficking mainly covers the common border of Bangladesh and India. The total land border of Bangladesh covers 4510 kilometres. of this Bangladesh has 288 kms common border with Myanmar (Burma). The rest, 4222 kms is with India alone. In total, 28 districts O_2 of Bangladesh have common border with India. The other two districts border with Myanmar. The geographical situation and economic background play an important role in trafficking.

Besides the land route the second most frequented route is the sky route. Women and children are being trafficking either on a work permit or a false family visa to distant countries, particularly in the Middle East. Being a developing country, economic hardships can be stated as a major cause of trafficking. Besides this cause, the investigation report of the Bangladesh National Women's Lawyers' Association (BWLA) focuses on several other facts.

The Bangladesh National Women's Lawyers' Association's border investigation report shows that:

- In 1947, as a result of the partition between India and Pakistan, many families were divided. Families that have relatives in India, especially Hindu families, regularly cross the border in order to visit them. The smugglers and traffickers are taking advantage of such persons and routes, with the help of certain members of the law enforcing agencies on each side of the border. Illegal border crossing is a burning question in the political arena. It is not possible to eliminate this problem in one year only by one organization, but we have been able to point out the problems and we are receiving thorough information regarding the matter.

- There are 50 Bangladeshi enclaves in India and 85 Indian enclaves in Bangladesh. The governments of the two countries have very little control over these areas. These enclaves are used as centres for smuggling and human trafficking. We are getting continuous reports from these enclaves. We were able to draw the attention of the Home

Ministry on the matter.

- There are 66 camps of stranded Pakistanis in 14 districts of Bangladesh. Though existing law restricts their movement outside the country, the 'Pakistanis' are crossing the border often. They maintain links with the smuggling and trafficking rings. They get a share on the price of the women and children sold in Pakistan and India.

Trafficking in women and children has become a multi-million dollar business in Bangladesh. It is very easy to traffick poverty - stricken women and children by alluring them with money and promises of employment abroad. On the other hand, the poor males are used as tools in accomplishing such a job. In Bangladeshi society, women are often neglected, and shunned for transgressing strict social values and norms. These 'rejected' women become easy prey for the traffickers. The street children are also easily persuaded to cross the border.

The desperate economic situation in Bangladesh, combined with oppression that many Bangladeshi girls suffer at the hands of their husbands and families, makes the country a favoured target of traffickers. Most of these girls trafficked into Calcutta are from poor Muslim families that often include several wives and a large number of children. Some of them, still in their early teens, might be pushed into work despite their lack of training and education; others might be married at that age. The ones who are married off usually have at least one or two children while they are still children themselves. The polygamous family system, characteristic of impoverished Muslim communities are plagued by physical abuse and desertion by husbands. Such women need to support themselves and their children and being uneducated and untrained to work they fall prey to various ploys used by the traffickers. The traffickers approach either the head of poor families or abandoned wives with children with the false offer of jobs and marriage. The traffickers, at times, simply kidnap young boys and girls and take them away through the borders. If the traffickers lure women with children then they get children as bonus with a woman.

It is ironical that at times when women are offered "good jobs" abroad the traffickers ask them to pay for their travel expenses. In this way, women themselves pay for being trafficked. Such instances occurred with women working, e.g., in garment factories, who hand over their savings to these criminals for their travel out of the country.

Law Relating to Trafficking in Bangladesh

The issue regarding trafficking in women and children has been incorporated into various Acts and laws of Bangladesh. The following laws/Acts deal with the manifestations associated with the evils of trafficking:

(a) Penal Code, 1860; (b) The Suppression of Immoral Trafficking Act, 1933; (c) Cruelty to Women Ordinance, 1983; (d) Women and Child Repression (Special Provisions) Act, 1995 and; (e) Articles 31 and 32 of the Constitution of Bangladesh.

Under the Penal Code, offences affecting the human body are punishable. The Penal Code of 1860 provides following punishable offences:

(a) Wrongful confinement (sections 342-346); (b) kidnapping or abduction from Bangladesh and kidnapping from lawful guardianship (sections 360-363); (c) abducting or kidnapping a person under the age of ten, or abducting a woman to compel her into marriage etc.; (d) eighteen years for sexual intercourse, (section 366A); (e) importation of girls from a foreign country; (f) buying of minors for purposes of prostitution etc. (section 373); (g) unlawful compulsory labour (section 374); and (h) rape (section 376). The penalty ranges from one year to ten years' imprisonment depending on the degree and intensity of the offence.

The Suppression of Immoral Trafficking Act, 1933, provides for punishment for forcing a girl under the age of 18 into prostitution. Abetment by one having custody or charge of the girl is also a crime. Section 11 of the Act provides a penalty of maximum three years of imprisonment or fine, or both.

The Women and Children Repression (Special Provisions) Act,

1995, section 8 provides a maximum penalty of life imprisonment and fine for the traffickers. It debars the granting of bail to persons accused of committing such an offence. The penalty imposed by section 9 of this Act for abduction of women and children to commit immoral acts is ten years', with minimum of seven years, imprisonment.

Articles 31 and 32 of the Constitution of Bangladesh state that: (31) To enjoy the protection of the law, and to be treated in accordance with law, and only in accordance with law, is the inalienable right of every citizen, wherever he may be and of every other person for the time being within (32). No person shall be deprived of life or personal liberty save in accordance with law.

I am happy to note that the Centre for Women-Children Studies (CWCS), Bangladesh has drawn up a scheme to ensure support to the victims of trafficking. The CWCS has taken an initiative to launch a *Trafficking Violence HELPLINE for Women and Children* as an outcome of the deliberations. CWCS will be the secretariat to carry out the operation of the *HELPLINE* with the support of concerned organizations.

6

Paedophilia: Adult's Satisfaction and Child's Agony!

At the climax of a drunken house party in Calcutta, the chosen invited guests were called to watch a pornographic video. "Its to add spice to the party!" the host exclaimed. To nearly everyone's shock, its contents were child pornography. To some people's shocked disbelief, its commentary and background evidenced that it was filmed somewhere in Mumbai. By the end of the party, a few of the visitors who were still around left their contacts in order to get their hands on that tape or a similar one.

> **The age range of the children in the video was between four and ten years. The fact must be stressed that these were prepubescent children. The title of this short-thirty minutes video was 'Ride On Me'.**

India today is at a crossroads and the edge of paedophilia. This kind of practice is slowly growing. Child abuse has been prevalent since quite some time but filming child abuse is a recent phenomenon. Paedophile really means "Filming of sexual acts with minors" and these films really involve children of as early ages as nine months old. Their age could be younger. It involves children having sexual intercourse with men, sexual objects like vibrators, sex with animals and also sex among themselves. Some children who are even still in nappies have the nappies removed, then intercourse begins. The terror and look in a child's eyes is sickening. The children scream very loudly during sex. All these acts are captured on film. Some of these children are boys with penetration occurring at the rear end. Moaning usually occurs from the adult while the child is screaming and whimpering. The adult finishes the act in satisfaction while the child is in pain and agony. Like in every society, our society would look at such horrendous acts with horror.

All of us are guilty of watching sexual films, reading sexual literature. We dress in a way that is provocative. The advertisements on television attract us by their sexual overtones in dress and talk. If we are bored with our sex life, we go to sex shops. Today's songs consist of so much unplicit or covert sex talk .... the list goes on. Casual sex is the biggest form of social acceptance today. With today's globalisation, its sexual culture is spreading from the 'superior culture' to the 'inferior culture'.

Sexual abuse of children has existed within close family members in homes. Very many children, especially girls have experienced some kind of sexual abuse but since our culture does not give a vent to talk about it, nor are the girls allowed to report the incidents due to cultural taboos and upbringing, the secret is nursed till death.

I recently presided over a conference where approximately a hundred adult delegates were present. We asked the delegates to close their eyes and press the button if on reflecting they remember to have been subjected to sexual abuse as a child in the family and to our surprise 98 buttons clicked to show the horror of sexual abuse within the family.

Many of the children involved in this abuse run away from home. They usually get involved in wrong acts due to lack of parental counselling, advice and control. These same children are used, exchanged or sold like the little girl who was sold in Pune in exchange for a small house. I met this little child in the Goa Bal Niketan. We had been informed by an NGO group working on children's issues, that a nine year-old girl, named Suku Bai Chandni had been rescued from the clutches of a Swiss man, and was housed in the Bal Niketan.

We met this little nine-year old. Bright, chirpy and radiant, little Suku Bai excitedly rattled to us that her "Uncle" (Swiss man) used to be very kind to her, gave her goodies to eat, lovely dresses to wear and lots of money to her invalid father who begs on the streets of Pune. Recently, a house was also purchased in Yervada, and given to her father. The Swiss man is a Rajneesh disciple. He kept Suku Bai for almost nine months with him, during which he also took her to Mumbai and they stayed in a hotel named 'Gulistan'. Suku innocently admitted that the foreigner used to caress her. He used to bathe her and fondle her. In the evenings everyday she would see blue films and he would caress her, kiss her and so on. At night he would tell her frightening stories, which naturally made the girl cling to him for security and he would then make her sleep close to him. From the experiences that Suku Bai shared with us, it was quite clear that the foreigner had been sexually playing with her, though he may not have actually penetrated her. However, it did come across that the girl seemed to want to go back to him, since in her innocence she seems to have got used to his playing around. He had taken lots of her poses on film.

By the time the girl realized what was happening to her. He would have claimed her as his own property and would have used her in any way he liked. The vicious circle diversifies child pornography and paedophilia. On the streets we find more boys than girls because there is a bigger market for the girls. One important question we ask is, "How big is this problem?" Statistics are very unreliable in this case because for one, such a problem has not come into the light; secondly, we do not have an effective police force to infiltrate this plague, as most of the members of police expressed their ignorance; thirdly, abused children rarely speak out about their experiences for fear of embarrassment and the stigma that attaches to such experiences.

We arrived in Panjim on 20th February 1997. As the objective of this visit was to accertain for ourselves the presence and extent of child prostitution and paedophilia, we surveyed two beaches, namely Baga and Calangute.

First we visited Baga. The beach as usual had large numbers of foreign tourists. As we drove down, we noticed that on the road leading to this beach, there were vendors on either side selling clothes, beads and trinkets. The girls vending were all young Lambani girls. We noticed several foreign tourists conversing with these young girls. We also saw a couple of foreigners, quite elderly men walking along with these young girls, several of whom were minors. Apparently it seemed, that under the garb of selling their wares, these girls were being prostituted.

On the beach, however, we did not see much activity as it was afternoon and the sun was scorching. Even the shacks were quite vacant. We were told that often deals are clinched in these shacks, and activity is at its peak in the evenings. The other beach that we visited was Calangute. This beach is on the tourist stop, and therefore you find lots of Indian as well as foreign tourists. On the beach here we met with a couple of little children, between 7-10 years, both girls and boys. The girls were selling trinkets and the boys fruits. We met four children and all of them were non-Goans. The two girls were from Agra and Gwalior, while the boys were from Bijapur, Karnataka.

The girls shared information with us that often foreign men accosted them, and offered them chocolates, gifts and clothes, they also said that the foreigners paid them much more for their wares compared to others. Well, explicitly they did not mention that foreigners sexually used them, but certainly in there innocent way, stated that they do fondle them and took many photographs of them in different positions.

The children very clearly mentioned that they were scared of the police, who harassed them. In fact, we were witness to this, when a cop came swinging his lathi, the children fled to hide themselves. Later when we called out to them assuring them that the cops will not catch them in our presence, they felt reassured and came out of hiding. The girls also told us that the police catch them, take them to the lock-up, where they are kept for a couple of days, during which they are hired out to men, who come in search of young girls, the men mostly being tourists.

With great difficulty, a ten-year-old pre-pubescent finally agreed to an interview. She related that she is involved in child sex sale and child pornography. To protect her identity, her name will be Asha. Asha admitted to having been in this trade for a few months. She was a tragic victim on account of being an orphan. Her aunt brought her to Mumbai where the city life and glamour excited her. Her first experience was scary. All was fine until one day her aunt took her to the home of a man and left her there, assuring her that the man would give her money if she agreed to do *nice* things with him. "He undressed me, started touching me, while closing his eyes and breathing heavily. He put me on him and pushed me down slowly. It was painful but he kissed me and gave me sweets and toffees. I was washed and cared for in that house by Aunty". Now Asha is not scared. She says it is okay. Asha claims most of her customers are "young boys and older men. They are sometimes big and fat".

"I cried once when a man did it in the back. It was so painful but I'm okay". Asked whether this was a normal lifestyle for her, she replied in the affirmative. She says there are a few other girls like her she has met. Now she is provided with accommodation and she gets money. "Aunt takes most of the money." Asked whether she has been filmed, she says "only two times". To Asha, like any other girl, this is an ordinary life. To another ten-year-old, whose life revolves around school, friends, parental love and prayers, Asha's life revolves around sex, and more sex from strangers.

How many Ashas exist, within our society? Is this myth or reality? It is hard to find these Ashas because they are well protected by their pimps. Adult prostitution is condemned but it exists openly. There is no place where child sex sale nor its filming can be accepted in our society. There are laws that have been passed banning sex with children below the age of consent. Similarly, laws exist banning the manufacture, distribution and possession of pornographic films. That, however, has not stopped the flow of these films nor has it limited its variety. Most films that are exchanged are between paedphiles and child molesters without any commercial motive. The ever-advancing film technology has made it easier. Paedophiles can now use the video camera to get his ends without involving the middle agent in the film processing. This agent eliminates all possible footage that is likely to be detected. Free of this, paedophiles copy their own material, cut it, edit it, insert titles and sound effects. Once done, the finished merchandise is exchanged with the underground world. And thereafter the observation as happened at the Calcutta house party.

Child pornography floods the outside market. This makes the Indian market feel amateurish. But even amateurs become experts. Now is the time to cry out before the situation gets completely out of hand. So given the above shocking revelations about these horrendous acts of child abuse and traumatisation, we as parents, brothers, sisters, relatives, friends and concerned citizens, have a moral duty to speak out against this monstrous and abhorrent trend that is eating into the vitals of our society like cancer, depriving these youngsters of their childhood and innocence. We must expose these evil acts and their perpetrators using the public media, the Press, the voices of our MPs and concerned citizens and any other effective means. We must enlist the help of the law-enforcers, sensitize the public about these goings-on and keep alert at all times about suspicious and shady characters and places, red-light streets as they are called. Every citizen owes it to the future generation of our country, to protect and ensure that it grows up in a healthy and desirable environment.

7

The Insatiable Lust of Man

Before putting forth the ways to tackle any problem or issue one must reach out to the roots of the problem. The causes for prostitution are multifarious and discussed by many authors but before presenting them in this chapter we must realize what are the factors that project the young children with the invisible tag that says "these children are vulnerable and available for abuse / exploitation". Though this tag is not seen by any sane person or society yet it is very well read by abusers, exploiters and traffickers.

We surveyed factors responsible for child trafficking and assessed the various mechanisms and mode of procuring children for trafficking, trafficking routes and destinations. We also identified the sectors of the society being the stakeholders in the trafficking chain—both those who seek financial gains and those who are implicated.

The question therefore is what are the causes of increase the number of child prostitutes almost everywhere, in India and elsewhere—in every part of the globe wherever there are human settlements and any semblance of civilization, sex with a child is rape—an offence. Even though being a blot on the face of humanity, it does persist.

The possible factors, which I have analysed are:

(a) general degeneration in human values leading to moral degrading; here it is important to point out that brothels are no longer run by pimps only. The operators now could also be a serving police officer, politician or a businessman;
(b) the role of media—especially the electronic media leading to indecent exposure of girl's anatomy;
(c) perversion;

(d) increase in use of alchohol and other toxicants;
(e) the false belief that sex with young girls may add years to one's lifespan—such beliefs being more predominant in people living in feudalistic environs and moffusil areas;
(f) the superstition that sex with a young girl may cure sexually transmitted diseases;
(g) the belief that in having sex with young girls there is little danger of HIV infections;
(h) the ease with which a young girl can be trapped and initiated into the vice with little fear of her complaining against her tormentors because of elements of fear and social stigma attached.

As I feel, the last factor is the motivator in most of the cases along with the general degeneration in consciousness leading to low morals. However, the underlying major cause is poverty, which in turn compels families to migrate and its worst consequences fall on women and children. Poverty and exploitation combine to make girls and women cheap commodities. Population explosion, low literacy levels, low skill-building opportunities, denial of access to resources, diminishing common property and vulnerability to natural calamities have compelled the rural poor to migrate to the cities. When the rural poor migrate to cities, traffickers take full advantage of their helplessness and lure their children with promises of money and jobs. Moreover, in the wake of the AIDS epidemic, younger girls and children are being sought for sex in the belief that they are less likely to be infected.

Firstly, discrimination of sex and oppression of the girlchild within the family, e.g., incest, is a cause enough to push the girls to look for alternate emotionally secure environment. Secondly, the disadvantaged position of girls within the Indian family that considers particularly expedient hasty child marriage in order to marry off daughters creates the perfect condition for those who profit from the labour of prostitutes.

Thirdly, girls who are abandoned by their husbands at a very young age with children are easy target for traffickers. Fourthly, ill-treatment within the family of any kind also predisposes a girl child to strike out on her own and seek the city thereby falling prey into the hands of traffickers.

Then, traffickers also look out for children who belong to broken families where either the parent is alcoholic or violent or the parents have separated and a single parent lives with another partner who may not necessarily be a good guardian to the child. These relationships coupled with poverty and stress due to living conditions, induce children to seek stability elsewhere.

The children of families where both the parents are working and stay out of the house for the whole day leaving their children behind are equally at risk of being abused. At times, children get lured due to lack of attention and affection and need to belong to someone. An exploiter gets involved with the family by giving them gifts and money in the guise of helping them. Unfortunately, these vulnerable children yearn for small comforts and thus develop a soft corner, allowing himself/herself to be exploited.

Children who run away on their own, suffer a raw deal. Lack of parental and societal protection, coupled with the need to be cared for, makes them vulnerable to the abusers. The young girls are often defenceless, dependent or destitute and are sexually assaulted by even close relatives or neighbours. The people, especially menfolk, from remote rural villages migrate to big cities for employment thereby exposing their families to the traffickers who take full advantage of their abject poverty and lure their children into the profession with promises of money and jobs.

The Causes of Prostitution

The causes of prostitution can be broadly categorized under the following categories :

1. Economic
2. Social
3. Cultural
4. Psychological
5. Self-rejection
6. Others.

Economic Reasons

Under this category poverty plays the major role in perpetuating this trade. Poverty marginalizes the victims and their families and often prevents them from seeking help and justice. It makes children easy prey and also forces the families of victims to be helpless enough to ignore the consequences of abuse. Due to the lack of viable alternatives for employment and sustenance, children of the poor are often pushed into prostitution to earn a livelihood for themselves and their families. Parents with large families or with more number of daughters are coerced to induct their daughters in the trade to earn extra money. Then, prevalence of dowry system does not always enable the parents to marry off their daughters. When traffickers approach them at this juncture parents are only too happy to wash their hands off their daughters. In one instance a father of six daughters was found guilty of selling his eldest daughter. The daughter pleaded with the officials and social workers to let her carry on with the sex trade so as to save the five other girls from stepping into her shoes. Poverty and exploitation combine to make girls and women a cheap commodity.

Social Factors

This category comprises of a number of perpetuating factors. The most common social cause is desertion by spouse. In our patriarchal society, man having an upper hand often desert the woman after staying with her for a short time. The case of child marriage has been mentioned earlier, where teenage mothers are left on their own by their husbands who in turn start staying with another woman. Thereafter, men woo young girls and when they have satisfied their sexual urge, they simply abandon that girl or may pass her into the hands of traffickers or exploiters. At times these men blackmail the girls and force them to continue the trade. The girls having illicit relationships also land in this trade whether voluntarily or involuntarily.

Traffickers, at times, deceive the girls with false promises of jobs and money in another place. This ploy is often used by traffickers to bring the girls from Nepal, Bangladesh and remote areas of India to big metropolitan cities like Delhi or Mumbai, etc. The girls who have been dejected in love by their paramours also fall easily into the trap laid by the traffickers. Sometimes due to death of head of family, the older girls, at a young age, have to earn livelihood for the family. Being unskilled, uneducated and understanding the gravity of the situation she has no other option but to jump in the fray so as to feed the hungry mouths back at home.

Prohibition of remarriage of widows who are young also plays its own role as a cause for prostitution. These young widows are always under pressure exerted by their brother-in-laws or other male members of the family and the neighbourhood. As they are not financially independent they are always considered a liability and a loathsome burden on the family and hence are ill-treated by men and women alike. This compels them to find support for themselves and at times, results in their joining the trade.

Cultural and Traditional Practices

The traditional and cultural practice of dedication of girls to gods and goddesses in temples plays an important role in promoting child prostitution as has been discussed earlier in case of Devadasis, Bogams, Jogins, Basavis, Murlis, etc. The practice of prostitution has been accepted as a tradition in few tribal communities such as Bedias, Bancharas, Rajnat, etc. as a result of economic oppression in some tribes, and as a tradition in others as also discussed earlier.

Psychological Reasons

Girls with psychological causes join the trade voluntarily. These girls are mostly exposed to and influenced by media and films. They are young aspirants who want to be rich and fulfil their ambitions within a quick span of time. They are driven by the desire for physical pleasure and a luxurious life. They have increasing craze for money which they want to earn by easy means. Such girls, usually fall in bad company at an early age in comparison to their peer group.

Self-rejection

The Indian society is characterised by wide variations in socio-cultural and economic conditions. The social structure is woven around the family, the community and the State. These institutions have traditionally been providing a protective umbrella and security to children in situations of distress, calamity or crisis. But there is, now, a definite change discernible in the pattern of family and community life, especially in the wake of socio-economic transition that the country has been undergoing. The process of change has accelerated with ideological and technological developments of the modern age. While the joint family system is yielding in favour of the nuclear family, individual life is being influenced more by economic interests than familial ties. Indeed, the unprecedented pace of industrialisation and consequential urbanisation have been the major factors in the transformation of the social milieu that the children are growing in. The accent on economic growth has led to various far-reaching changes in population structure, social mobility and communication. A large number of people are migrating from rural areas to urban centres, mainly in search of gainful vocations and betterment of their living standards. Most of these poor migrants have to struggle for sheer survival, in a situation of social marginality. This trend is often associated with total disruption of their family and community ties, of which children are the worst victims. Boys and girls who feel that they are not appreciated or loved at home develop hostile and defiant attitudes towards parents as also towards all those in authority. They become disobedient, troublesome and unruly because of the unfavourable attitude towards them in the immediate environment. At times this might become a way of life when such adverse circumstances are buttressed by poverty, lack of proper guidance and support and consequently the children become victims of anti-social elements as also the agents of prostitution.

Such persons become self-rejectants when they are unable to gratify their needs and desires. This in turn lead them to dislike themselves and be unhappy resulting in maladjustment in their day-to-day living.

On the many causes of self-rejection the following are the most common and damaging:

1. Unrealistic expectations
2. Environmental obstacles

3. Unfavourable social attitudes
4. Personal limitations
5. Identification with maladjusted people
6. Inability to get a proper self-perspective
7. Poor childhood training
8. Lack of motivation
9. Severe emotional strain
10. Repeated failures

Within this framework, let us understand the psychosocial, cultural and economic interiors of child prostitution in India.

Other Factors

This category comprises of different isolated factors. When the traffickers are unable to use any foul play they simply abduct the child from outside her / his house. The children thus kidnapped are of tender age who are unable to put any resistance or identify them or their whereabouts and could easily be moulded in whatever shape the traffickers wants to give them.

As mentioned earlier, men from the rural areas migrate to bigger cities for employment as more opportunities are available in bigger town due to industrialization. In this way they are away from their wives and home and hence visit prostitutes to satisfy their biological urge consequently increasing the demand of prostitutes. Similarly, there are certain other vocations like those of salesmen, truck drivers, tourists, busdrivers, travelling agent of many companies, etc. who live away from home for several days and even months. Thousands of unmarried young men have to live away from home studying or working in distant towns. They might, at times, for curiosity's sake try to visit a prostitute just for an experience. They are the people who create a demand for prostitutes and make all sorts of efforts to obtain her services.

However, an interesting development is underway in the red-light areas of the megapolises of our country. The women already inducted into the profession in these areas realise that it is the only livelihood they are going to be allowed to indulge by society. But they also want to revolt against the monetary exploitation. As a result they no longer consider it profitable to function as brothel inmates since the major portion of the money goes to the brothelkeepers. So many of them have started functioning as call girls. While this option is available to women in towns and cities, in rural areas, the women in prostitution are still largely from communities that have been traditionally engaged in entertainment.

With the advent of tourism in the late 19th century trafficking in human beings has become an international phenomenon. Tourism has received a fresh impetus in the era of globalisation. Child pornography, the fear of AIDS, paedophiles, and the vulnerability of people in tourist destinations like Thailand, Sri Lanka, the Philippines and now also India, has encouraged sex tourism that mainly targets women and children (boy and girls alike) in these countries.

About a year back over 300 Sri Lankan migrant women workers were stranded on account of being variously duped at the Sri Lankan embassy in Kuwait at the start of September. One hundred and forty-one of them were brought back to the country on 24th September, 1997 and sent back to their respective hometowns.

Most of the women returnees alleged that their agents had abandoned them once they faced difficulties at their places of employment. Some of the women returnees suffered abusive beatings, while others claimed that they had not been paid promised wages and were sexually exploited. Some of them had not received any wages at all. Almost all of them complained of long hours of work and abusive treatment. The women had sought protection at the Sri Lankan embassy in Kuwait as they could not afford to purchase a ticket to return home.

Likewise, thousands of Burmese women and girls are trafficked into Thai brothels every year where they work under conditions tantamount to slavery. Subject to debt bondage, illegal confinement, various forms of sexual and physical abuse and exposure to HIV in the brothels, they then face wrongful arrest as illegal immigrants if they try to escape or if the brothels are raided by Thai police. Once arrested, the women and girls may be subjected to further sexual abuse in Thai detention centres. They are then taken for deportation to the Thai-Burmese border where they are often lured back into prostitution by brothel agents who play on their fear of arrest on return to Burma. Thai police and border patrol officials are involved in both the trafficking and brothel operations.

In a bid to earn more and more foreign exchange, tourism is being encouraged by the government irrespective of the problems naturally associated with the growth of unchecked tourism. Ever since the governments in Sri Lanka, Thailand and the Philippines have tightened laws, there is evidence which suggests that sex tourists have set their eyes on tourist destinations in India. Earlier it was Goa and now Kovalam beaches of Karela and Paradeep ports in Orissa are fast developing as paradise for sex tourists.

The main cause which promotes child prostitution is that the people en masse are generally ignorant and illiterate. Parents as well as children are absolutely uneducated, unskilled and burdened with the responsibility of supporting others in the family. This characteristic of the vulnerable group creates a situation wherein either they are fully exploited by traffickers or they are forced to join the profession on their own. When girls of this group are trafficked into another province/city/country they are unable to find their way back and with no alternative continue in the trade endlessly.

Another main cause for the increase in demand for young girls is the myth (as mentioned earlier) that intercourse with a virgin can cure a man of sexually transmitted diseases and rejuvenate him. It is also a widely prevalent though erroneous belief that sex with a girlchild does not expose the man to STDs and HIV. As the threat of AIDS mounts and it becomes the largest killer disease, child prostitutes have become the largest carriers of the deadly HIV virus. It is well-known fact that generally girls do not enter the trade themselves. Usually, some other persons are is responsible for their induction into the trade.

Means used by Traffickers

The means commonly used by traffickers to induct girls and women into prostiuttion include allurement of work, Posing as relative/fake guardianship, by force blackmailing, fake friendship, false marriage, kidnapping and rendering senseless by using drugs.

Persons responsible for induction of girls into the trade are usually someone close to the girl. It has been seen that under stress some parents themselves introduce the girl into the trade. The girls who have been married at an early age or are abandoned are eyed by their brothers-in-law who wants to take advantage of their adverse situation. Thereafter goonda elements takeover and are always on the look out for young lonely girls. At times, neighbours deliberately get friendly with the girl's family and lure away the girls into the trade. Sometimes, old prostitutes return to their native place and show off their wealth to attract young ambitious girls and induce them to take the easy path to earn more money. These old prostitutes may be distant relatives of the girl's family but still do not hesitate to exploit the girl. At times, deals are struck with the parents themselves. Girls are coaxed to join the trade by their friends who are already working in this profession.

When the girls start working in this trade it may not be necessary that they work in total secrecy all the time. They might even work with the consent of either mother, sister or even brothers or at times even the whole family. In such cases, the girls are accepted in the family in contrast to the ones who are abducted and pushed into the trade with no fault of their own.

8

Legalization of Prostitution: To be or not to be

At the National Commission for Women in the capacity of Chairperson I initiated long discussions on the subject of women in prostitution and found a consensus that society's focus was constantly on the changes and reform that was expected of these women, but in contrasts, the reality was that it was society's responses and attitudes that had to change drastically if at all these women had to be helped.

I resolved then to directly meet as many women as I could. This journey took me from the narrow streets of Benaras, through Orissa, Andhra Pradesh, Karnataka, Maharashtra, Uttar Pradesh, Madhya Pradesh, Manipur, Sikkim, Assam, Goa, West Bengal, Bihar and Kerala where I met more than 80,000 women in various situations and circumstances and heard them speak "openly, without fear, and with hope."

Throughout my discussions with various women and children the foremost request was that they should be treated as equal citizens of India. As the Chairperson I also agreed that we do not want the traditional *soft options* for these women. I strongly felt that their requirements and concerns be set out firmly in all the developmental issues.

During those discussions I recognised the major role and value of collectivism and the building of cooperative self-help spirit and institution among the women in prostitution. This we found to be an important first step towards change both for themselves and the violence within the societies which contain and perpetuate these systems. Although the wisdom of Chanakya can be related here calling this profession an "invisible profession", an attempt has been made nowadays to make this group of women visible. The question is would this visibility jeopardize their existence?

I personally chose to hear these thousands of voices in the hope of evoking appropriate responses and capture the landscape of prostitution in the country in the hope of analysing the issue. Hence today the hottest debate among women's groups is whether to legalize this profession or not. Today most of the women activists seek answers to this question in meetings, seminars, conventions and national consultations.

During all my visits to the various meetings in the red light areas I asked the women, "Daughter, what is it you want"? and in each of these meetings the answers were always "Ma, I don't want my daughter to be in this profession. Please take her away and keep her in a boarding school". Hence I do believe that no prostitute really thinks that this could be a dignified profession for her child – and leads me to conclude that really speaking they would not like legalization.

Article 19(1) (g) of the Constitution says : "All citizens shall have the right to practise any profession, or to carry on any occupation, trade or business." And in Article 21: "No person shall be deprived of his life or personal liberty except according to procedure established by law. "The group demanding legalization quotes from the above two Articles and calls upon the fundamental rights of every citizen to practise any profession he/she may choose.

The most vocal among groups advertising legalization of prostitution is the Mahila Samanwaya Committee, Calcutta. They held two conferences of the National Network of Sex Workers at Salt Lake Stadium in Calcutta in March, 1998 perhaps it was for the first time that the sports stadium hosted a conference on prostitution. It was attended by 1600 sex workers including 12 delegates of the Asia-Pacific Network of Sex Workers. The conference *inter alia* discussed issues like depcriminalisation of prostitution through repeal of the Prevention of Immoral Traffic Act, legal recognition of trade and of sex workers as workers and their right to form a trade union, a self-regulatory board to allow sex workers to gain control over their own work and also to prevent entry of minor girls into flesh trade. The sex workers declared that they earned their bread from manual work and as such wanted to be recognised as industrial labourers. They did not want any more girls to be tricked into the profession.

It was generally felt that sex workers still remain outcasts and untouchables according to conventional morality. They were even denied the attention that slum dwellers received. It was time now that they were freed of the long-time ignominy heaped upon them. Legalisation of sex workers would help contain child prostitution, forced prostitution, Devadasi system besides reducing atrocities at the hands of mafia and police and as also would help maintain their health.

During the conference several resolutions were passed and at the end of the conference the sex workers' organisations decided to approach MPs to get their profession recognised. They also wanted favourable material to be prepared to put up a case for the sex workers' rights. A public opinion survey conducted during the Calcutta Book Fair, 1998 held from 28th January to 8th February, 1998, in which 525 persons most of them educated, responded, was also released. It revealed that over 80 per cent of those who responded accepted that the profession should be legalised and sex workers must also enjoy equal rights. Seventy three per cent of the respondents opined that children of sex workers should be known by their mother's identity. About the motive behind police raids, a large section of the respondents (72.6 per cent) opined that police conducted raids primarily to harass the sex workers as it was the easiest way for the police to extort money.

At a national meeting of the National Commission for Women held at Delhi in 1996 an idea to form a collective to safeguard the interests of women in prostitution was mooted. While the concept of such collectives is in its infancy in India, the women who are its members are learning how to negotiate with society and earn a dignified place for themselves. Shabana from Nippani is part of VAMP or Veshya AIDS Muqabla Parishad which is a collective of women in prostitution. She said, "Now that we women can work on our own, we shall ourselves solve our problems instead of running to someone else. Our collective gives us a powerful identity as also the means to fight the problems connected with sex work and we are gaining in confidence."

At first they could not believe that they could come together as a result of a collective which was formed in 1996. The Chittoor Mahila AIDS Control Sangham (CMACS) was registered as a collective of sex workers with the aim of promoting the health and welfare of women. This organisation has given tremendous confidence and strength to the women. In some cases, the need for collective has stemmed from dissatisfaction with the NGOs working with women in prostitution. It was felt that the NGOs were representing their own interests and not those of the women they were working for. Lata was deserted by her husband when she was sixteen and later sold into a Mumbai brothel. She says: "We do not need NGOs to speak on our behalf, they are a big problem. We are doing real social work ourselves, interacting with the community, spreading awareness about AIDS, distributing condom, conducting health programmes and releasing women from unlawful custody".

It was felt that the presence of a self-regulatory board would go a long way in solving the problem. It should be constituted with a specified number of sex workers and non-sex workers — professionals like doctors, legal experts, etc. This board should control the trade. The advantages of such a board, the participants felt, would be:

(a) Forcing women into the trade would be restricted.
(b) The middlemen would not be able to demand large kickbacks.
(c) One would enter the trade with a fuller knowledge of it.
(d) The board could deal with grievances particularly those arising out of members of police and medical community.
(e) A model code of conduct could be laid down by the board.
(f) Such a board will be effective in preventing the entry of underage girls in the trade.
(g) The board can make the use of condoms mandatory.
(h) A recognised profession and a recognised trade will protect from exploitation by police.

(i) The self -regulatory board will be the first stepping stone in the sex worker's quest for more rights. The board will be a symbol of the legitimacy of their lives.

(j) Sex workers will have more control over their bodies if they have a board and can say 'no' to a client.

(k) The board will help to shield them from protection rackets run by landlords, the police and local thugs.

The group demanding legalization was of view that this will lead to acceptance of reality, will bring some rules and regulation for this section of women and will protect and safeguard them. Once legalized, the business of prostitution may be monitored and will discipline the defaulting houses. If legalized, the brothels could be isolated as an authorized place where whoever wants to utilize the services of a prostitute can do so without involvement of any middlemen. This group of activists believes that legalization will eliminate the involvement of pimps, brothelkeepers, madams, and traffickers. The woman practising prostitution will not be obliged to part with her income to this group of people who at present snatch a lion's share from her earnings. On the other hand, consequently, legalization will also reduce racketeering and forcing of minors into this vortex. The girls will no longer remain in the clutches of crime perpetuators nor will forever be bound to repay the "debt" they have not taken. Laws, thus enacted, would enable every woman practising prostitution to move the court if being bullied, assaulted, harassed or coerced by anti-social elements, pimps, clients or even police. If given a licence, all prostitutes could come together under the same umbrella and may form a union like any other to look after their rights. Their status as bonded labour will vanish.

Today, old as well as sick women are thrown out of brothels and have no place to go. Their families refuse to accept them, the government has no provision for such women anywhere and ultimately they go back to the profession and operate independently. Activists believe the important turn in their situation would be that they will have free access to medical services. Then, they will not sell their sick and tainted bodies to earn their livelihood. And, rehabilitation centres would be run and it would become obligatory to tend for old and sick sex workers in their difficult times.

Another section of women activists oppose the above arguments and are against legalization. Unlike as in the West, in our Indian society our culture, traditions and moral values taboo sex in the open or even talking about it in normal discussions among family members and even among friends. In Western countries, child-parent relationship is not as strong and so individuals, while growing up and during adolescence, seek emotional security and dependency among their peer groups or even elders resulting in weak and unstable relationships between boys and girls and subsequently men and women. This leads to free and open sex in the society and is very well accepted. But the same is not true in our country. Of course, the mentality of the younger generation along with moral values are fast changing in India but still the things are under the control of elders. People are more inclined to copy Western culture but at the same time they are not able to leave the Indian traditions behind absolutely. No doubt, though prostitution is a reality but it is accepted as a social evil.

Even if legalized, the women practising the trade will never be able to shake off the label and stigma of prostitution attached to them. Our society will still not accept them in mainstream. Even in the West, women with the label of prostitutes are not considered fit for the mainstream. The reason lies in the fact that prostitution is a clandestine profession and violative of the laws of society as well as of the country.

The group of women activists against legalization consider prostitution bad for the physical, mental, social and moral health of an individual and consequently of society. On the contrary, there is a widespread opinion of some educators and formatters of society that "prostitution acts as a sewage system for extra-seminal fluid in the society." The society is cleansed of the evil of rape and other sexual offences because of the existence of prostitution. It is ironical, that in today's environment when more and more individuals, especially children are being pushed into this trade each day to make prostitution legal, as it is now "a five billion dollar" industry, there is tremendous increase in sexual offences especially incest and rape of minors. At this rate where are we heading to? With both graphs showing consistent increase, will legalizing prostitution help reduce the agony of poor, vulnerable women and children? And the most important question currently being asked is will legalisation of the sex trade solve the problem of children? It is a general feeling that legalization will result in business being carried on both legally and illegally.

Do we give licence to smugglers, thieves and anti-social elements to do their job. If they start asking for licence to carry out their respective jobs which are equally illegal, will some or the other organization support them, ever. Then why should prostitution be legalized? Legalization would vitiate the moral atmosphere of the country. It would give anti-social elements the licence to indulge in trafficking and trade of humans. Do we legalize corruption? If we could legalize corruption we could as well legalize prostitution.

The group of women in favour of legalization hold the belief that it will reduce the incidence of HIV/AIDS and will act as a preventive measure for the spread of dreadful diseases as the women will have full rights and would be able to insist on safe sex. If the client does not agree she would have full right to turn him out. This seems very ideal but the example of Australia tells us otherwise.

When prostitution was legalized in Australia to obtain a licence the woman needed to have mandatory testing for HIV and certificate for disease-free body. An impact on society was felt as a large number of clients were attracted to legalized brothels. This practice, instead of preventing or reducing the spread of disease, led to increase in the number of HIV cases as it was customers who spread the disease than the prostitutes.

Many case-studies have been cited in the next few chapters where it is seen that young girls are introduced to the clients as virgins at a tender age. At the time of induction they are healthy but in about two years' time they are cases of full- blown dreadful diseases as STDs, tuberculosis, HIV/AIDS, etc. Who is responsible for their such condition? Again, it has happened because they are exposed to a large number of clients and have no right to insist on safe sex. In this condition either these girls are dumped or thrown out of the brothels with nowhere else to go. Will legalization solve the problem of such women?

Therefore, in gist whether prostitution should be legalized or not the arguments made for and against it are given in the table below:

Legalization of Prostitution

For	*Against*
1. The sex workers earn their bread from physical labour and therefore they should be recognised as industrial labourers/workers.	1. The demand is illegal, im moral, unethical and viola-tive of our constitu-tional provisions. The Constitution gives the choice of profession but does not permit indul-gence in socially undesirable activities.
2. A trade union will enable them to clinch their rights as workers, help them achieve some social acceptability and protect them from regular harassment by police and other forces. Prominent trade unions like AITUC, CITU, BMS, government employees unions and some women groups have promised to extend help to them.	2. Sex abuse is the worst form of violation of human rights.
3. Such a move would go a long way, to usher in the much needed improvements in the red-light districts.	3. Legalizing prostitution is not the remedy of the problem. The solution lies in rescuing and rehabilitating the women and children caught in the profession that offers no way out.
4. Countries like New Zealand, the Netherlands, Australia	4. It would give anti-social elements the licence to

and Bangladesh have already recognised prostitution.	indulge in the trafficking and trade of humans.
5. Such a step will pave the way for sex workers to form societies, improve their economic status and working conditions and prevent entry of minor girls in the profession.	5. It is mostly the poor and ignorant who are exploited and forced into trade. It is the duty of the government to prevent children from the marginalised section of society from being forced into the profession and to check perpetration of atrocities upon them.
6. Such a step will check sale of girls as there will be a board run by sex workers themselves to regulate the trade.	6. Prostitution leads to many life-taking diseases and once it is legalized, there will be a quantum jump in the spread of the diseases. Moreover, it is not a healthy occupation.
7. Such a step will also save women from AIDS and other venereal diseases because then they will be in a position to insist on safe sex.	7. The demand is being raised by people who are being funded by foreign donor agencies.
8. Legislation will also rescue and safeguard women from exploitative landlords and other exploiters.	
9. We have not been able to abolish prostitution for ages, so why not legalize and regulate it. Moreover it is not immoral because most of the sex workers are forced into it by the system and do not have a choice to either leave or accept it.	

Whether legalization to prostitution, is granted or not we are currently more concerned about the issue of children who are victims of paedophilia, trafficking, incest and rape at a very tender age of five years onwards. We have to rescue them, protect them and safeguard their interests to save them from their present agony and ensure a secure future for them.

9

Does Political Will Exist? Is it a Political Agenda?

Throughout my meetings, whether it be in Sweden, Bangladesh, Nepal or Pakistan the most important concern that came out again and again was the issue whether the political commitment or will was forthcoming? Hiding themselves under great traditions and ethical values, many old countries are practitioners of child prostitution. Almost all the countries in the region have been witnessing a growth in child rape and prostitution. It is a feature witnessed often around tourist and religious places as they are visited by migrants and floating population, particularly foreigners. According to a study nearly 30 per cent of prostitutes are below the age of 20. Many of the present-day prostitutes (40 per cent of them) entered the profession when they were children.

The issue of trafficking and commercial sexual exploitation of women and children or prostitution is gaining prominence in international circles, amongst NGOs, governments and concerned citizens. It has crossed international barriers and it is now a worldwide phenomena. Every year more than one million children worldwide are reportedly trafficked and sold for sexual abuse. Girls are forced into prostitution and denied basic human rights and dignity by the mental and physical abuse they have to endure. Poverty, illiteracy, cultural practices, money power, political forces, tourism and above all the girl's low status in society encourage and sustain her sexual exploitation. Each day victims of this trade face violence, intimidation, rape, torture from pimps, brothel-owners and even law enforcement agents. This sexual servitude is maintained through overt coercion, physical abuse, emotional blackmail, economic deprivation, social isolation and death threats.

In India, female prostitution has been recognised as an old and continuing social evil. It has faced moral disapproval all along, but is practised all the same by men and women. It is found in a concentrated manner in brothels and red-light areas. The more dispersed form may be found along major high-ways, in massage parlours, guest houses, call girl rackets, cabaret shows, female escort services, etc.

India and some other countries of the region are not wanting in theoretical formulations. There are several laws on the matter. But the major weakness seems to lie in the lack of sincerity in their execution and vigour in implementation of anti-prostitution measures.

The Male SAARC Summit, in July 1997 had expressed grave concern on the trafficking of women and children. "The Heads of State and of Governments pleaded to coordinate their efforts and take effective measures to address the problem. They decided that existing legislation in Member States should be strengthened and strictly enforced. This should include simplification of repatriation procedures for victims of trafficking. They also decided that the feasibility of establishing a regional convention on combating the crime of trafficking in women and children for prostitution has to be examined by the relevant technical committee. The Heads of Government urged India to prepare a working draft on the problem which is now sweeping the region and threatening to become one of the severest maladies of the future.

India has now prepared a working draft on how to combat trafficking in women and children for prostitution within SAARC countries. It will be placed for discussion at a meeting of experts group from SAARC member nations to be held in June, 1998, before the Regional Meeting. Preventing trafficking along borders, humanistic approach to rehabilitative care of victims, guidelines for repatriation and exemplary punishment to criminals who indulge in flesh trade are the major thrust areas proposed in the convention.

The government has also drawn up a list of source areas from where most prostitutes—adult or childre—originate and find their way into the flesh trade in metropolitan and other big cities. The high supply zones identified are Andhra Pradesh, Karnataka, Maharashtra, Tamil Nadu, Uttar Pradesh and West Bengal. According to a survey, 2.7 per cent of the prostitutes are from the Bangladesh region, 2.6 per cent are from Nepal, 0.3 per cent from Kuwait and 0.7 per cent from Tibet.

It is reported that young girls and women are being trafficked across well-beaten paths within South Asia and further afield. From just two routes—Nepal to India and Bangladesh to Pakistan involve an estimated 9,000 girls trafficked in a year. Though no recent estimates are available with the government, a sample survey done five years ago had estimated the number of child prostitutes at 15 per cent of the total population of prostitutes in the country.

Being in a unique position of both a receiving and transit nation, India's role in tackling the problem assumes greater significance. While concentrating on inter-State dealings, we have also had to keep the international ramifications in mind while making the first draft. Each country depending on its receiving or sending status would have specific requirements which too would be discussed at the meeting and incorporated in the final action plan.

Multilateral mechanisms like creating joint vigilance bureaus along the borders, constant monitoring and better enforcement of laws, appointing special trafficking officers with more enforcement and custodial officers and orienting and sensitising them to the problem, allowing the highest investigating agencies of the country like the Central Bureau of Investigation to handle inter-State, intra-regional and international trafficking are some of the proposals likely to find a consensus.

The Supreme Court of India in its verdict dated 9th July, 1997 directed Central Government and the State Governments to constitute a committee to make an in-depth study into the problem and evolve suitable schemes. The committee has already submitted its report along with an Action Plan. State Governments will be given directions for effective implementation of the schemes. A permanent Committee of Secretaries will review the progress of the implementation of the schemes evolved.

The action plan prepared by Central Government *inter alia* envisages educating the vulnerable groups, like destitute women and children and establishing contact centres at various places where they can seek help instead of falling into traps of anti-social elements.

Coordination among the Department of Tourism, Border Police and hotel managements in metro cities is also planned to check intra-State trade.

With the recent 73rd and 74th Amendmentts the Constitution, the functioning of the local self-governing institutions (Panchayati Raj in the villages and municipalities in the towns and cities) have been considerably strengthened. The women have emerged in public political sphere at decision-making level, with more powers and functions; they have thus been vested with more political and administrative efficacy. This is sought to be utilised to prevent trafficking in women and children. This is necessary, more so because according to many studies, the trade picks up innocent women languishing in poverty and search of jobs from the rural areas. Migration of women from rural to urban areas and their isolation and loneliness in the cities have also been responsible for this. The "missing" women and girls can be identified easily only at the local level. The local bodies, particularly the village level Panchayats are in a position to identify and prevent such occurrences. They can also help better in rescuing and rehabilitating the same.

No political party has an agenda in which prostitution figures as an item although everybody calls it a social evil and disgrace to civilization. If political parties are talking of equality, human rights, egalitarian society and civil liberty, why are they not, in their eloquent speeches, bringing in, the subject of prostitution and adding it in their manifestoes, for the elimination of commercial sex trade? Maybe because, politics is still dominated by men. Elimination of prostitution, for instance, goes against their male domination!

Hence, it can prudently be surmised that prostitution will continue in the world as long as man's domination continues in this world. Women rights are part of human rights. Women in bondage is a shame for a civilised society. Our actions, with all its hopes and all its efforts, can never really be free until the last and the least women among us is free from exploitation. Gandhiji had hoped and worked for feminising the political process equally with the males. He had a vision of clean and unsullied politics with women's equal participation. But after Independence, women in Parliament and politics could not keep themselves from emphasizing issues of women. They felt that they represent both men and women and were drawn into the game of power with all its ruthlessness.

After meeting several thousands of these children I have posed only one single question to the so-called civil society "will you please employ/educate this little girl who wants to get out from the brothel"? And the answer is always invariably of disbelief and shock, short of accepting such an idea. There has not been a single person in all my meetings in 384 districts who has volunteered to sustain these little girls honourably.

The National Human Rights Commission, India is also equally concerned over the menace of sexual exploitation of women and children. The Commission has called a meeting of all District Magistrates, Superintendents of Police and source communities to work out a concrete plan of action for prevention of child prostitution. It has also taken a decision to intensify action against child prostitution in Delhi and work out a long-term strategy for the rehabilitation of children rescued from prostitution. It has also appointed a core group to monitor the issue.

Bangladesh

So far as Bangladesh is concerned, the situation of women's empowerment is no better there than that of the other countries of the subcontinent. In most cases the situation is worse than in India. However, the Government of Bangladesh is trying to increase the women's political participation in different tiers of the power structure. At the same time different women's organizations are lobbying with the government and acting as pressure groups to realize their demands.

Government's Initiative to Empower Grass Roots Level Women

The Government of Bangladesh has taken an initiative to increase women's participation in policy planning and decision-making levels especially in Union Parisads — the lowest strata of local government in Bangladesh. In the past Union Parisad members nominated three female members. In accordance with the new regulations a union is divided into nine wards and one male member will be elected from every ward. At the same time every union comprising 9 wards has been divided into three parts for women members who will be elected through direct vote. After this change in electoral procedures a great enthusiasm had been noticed among the women candidates during the Union Parisad election which was held from 1st December to 31st December, 1997. It is regarded as a primary success on way to women's political empowerment in Bangladesh.

Government's Initiative of a Special Squad in the Criminal Investigation Department

The government has planned to set up a Special Squad in the Criminal Investigation Department to tackle the increasing problem of women and child trafficking in the country. A proposal in this regard was under scrutiny in the Home Ministry. The team will assist the police units whenever there is a report of any missing women or children. It will have direct contact with other countries through the interpol. Moreover, the squad will work closely with the NGOs to obtain information.

In this regard a task force has been set up to investigate into the incidents relating to trafficking in women and children. This has been stated by the Inspector General of Police, Mr Ismail Hossein in a seminar on "Role of Youths to Combat Trafficking in Women and Children" organized by the Rotary Club of Lalbagh Fort at the National Press Club in Dhaka on 30th March, 1998.

Excerpts of Address on the Issue of Trafficking in Women and Children by the Prime Minister of Bangladesh

The Honourable Prime Minister of the Government of the People's Republic of Bangladesh Sheikh Hasina expressed her deep concern over the increasing rate of trafficking in women and children in Bangladesh, reiterated the issue in Parliament, policy level gatherings and conferences of the law enforcing agencies. She declared this problem as a national concern. Recently, on March 10, 1998 on the occasion of National Standard Presentation and Golden Jubilee celebration of Ansar and Village Defence Party (VDP) she exhorted the members to play a more effective role in building up resistance against trafficking and women repression. She also emphasized the role of Ansars and VDP in containing this evil and said that their role is very much effective in raising awareness among the community.

Nepal

So far as Nepal is concerned, there has been a lack of a strong national policy relating to trafficking in girls for many years. Due to the strong pressure and advocacy from NGOs, the Ministry for Women and Social Welfare formed a National Task Force in March, 1997 to draft national plans and policies for the prevention trafficking of grils. The draft policy has been passed by the Cabinet. The highlights of the national policy are as follows:

1. For the prevention of trafficking, in girls the government will give greater emphasis to non-formal education, vocational education and employment-oriented programmes for the girls.
2. The government will form a National Coordination Committee for the prevention of trafficking of girls. Likewise, coordination committees will be formed at village and district levels according to need.
3. A district level information centre will be established with the objective to disseminate information on the issue of trafficking of girls.
4. The government will initiate poverty alleviation and employment generation programmes for women.
5. In view of the strong relationship between STDs and HIV/

AIDS and girls, trafficking, effective programmes will be launched to deal with the problem of HIV/AIDS.

6. The government will make arrangements to pay compensation to the victims from the exploiter.
7. To eliminate discrimination against women, new laws related to women will be formulated.
8. The government will establish bilateral and multilateral cooperation with other countries for the prevention of trafficking of girls.
9. Massive awareness campaigns will be launched by the government for the prevention of trafficking of girls.
10. Political commitment from all the political parties is indispensable for the prevention of trafficking of girls. So, the cooperation of all the political parties will be taken for the prevention programmes.
11. The Ministry for Women and Social Welfare will work as a focal point for the girls' trafficking prevention programmes.
12. The government will run integrated programmes involving the NGOs, private sector, and international organizations for the prevention of trafficking in girls.

Recently, the Ministry for Women and Social Welfare also entered into an agreement with the International Labour Organisation to work for the prevention of trafficking of girls. Some of the laws drafted by the Ministry, which will most probably be presented at the next session of Parliament, include laws against domestic violence and the establishment of a family court. The Ministry for Women and Social Welfare is also planning to run a home for the destitute and old women. It has also formed a coordination committee to draft a plan of action of independent Commission for Women. Recently the Ministry of Home Affairs has also entered into an agreement with UNICEF to train and mobilize police in the creation of awareness and prevention of trafficking.

The Ministry for Women and Social Welfare also organized a week-long training on gender and development to the Under Secretaries of the sectorial ministries. An orientation programme of GAD (Gender and Development) was also provided to the secretaries and joint secretaries. Recently, the government formed the National Coordination Committee with the Chairperson being the honourable minister. Similarly, District Coordination Committees will also be formed under the coordination of the district chairman.

It is due to the lack of awareness and low literacy rates that the majority of the girls are trafficked for prostitution. Therefore, the government has given more priority to girls' education. The key policies on education include massive awareness campaigns, as well as provision for a special incentives programme for girls from primary to higher education. In addition, there is also provision to appoint one female teacher in each of the primary schools in Nepal.

The most important thing in this regard is the concern of the Heads of States or Governments during the ninth SAARC Summit. Discussions took place to alleviate the situation of girls in especially difficult circumstances, including those orphaned, disabled and exploited as well as efforts to address the problem effectively. The directives of the Regional Convention on Combating the Crime of Trafficking Women and Children for Prostitution was also discussed in the twelfth meeting of the Committee on Women and Development, held in Kathmandu on 21-22 September, 1997.

For the past ten years the Ministry of Labour has also initiated some intervention programmes relating to trafficking. The ministry has been providing a 9-month skill development training to 25 women annually from the five areas prone to girls' trafficking. The training programme is designed mainly for the possible victims of trafficking. Previously, there was a lack of programmes for the rescued girls by the concerned ministry.

The other positive development by the government in favour of women and children is the ratification of the Convention on the Rights of the Child on 19th August, 1990 and also the ratification of the UN Convention on Eliminating all Forms of Discrimination against Women on 17th December, 1990. The promulgation of the new Constitution of the Kingdom of Nepal, 1990 also contains clauses of special benefit to children including rights to citizen ship, equality, education, a right against exploitation, and special protection for the disadvantaged, such as disabled children and orphans.

Pakistan

In Pakistan the issues noted there are sexual abuse of the girl child, trafficking in girls, prostitution, rape, custodial rape, sexual harassment at workplace and forced marriage of grown-up women as well as minor girls.

Most of the forms of sexual abuse of women are rooted in social tradition and custom as determined by a male-dominated feudal society. Poverty, lack of economic openings for the worst-off sections of society and denial to women of the status of economically productive members of society have strengthened these practices. Three recent factors have increased the incidence of women's sexual exploitation. First, the pseudo-Islamisation carried out by Gen. Zia (and also not discontinued by his successors) has made women more vulnerable by reinforcing the concept of women's inferior status, by loosening the redress mechanism in case of rape, and by strengthening forces that deny women independence in the choice of their spouses, share in family management and freedom to adopt vocations. Secondly, faced with breakdown of law and order, successive governments have enlarged the powers allowed to the police and other security forces. They have used this freedom as a licence to kill innocent citizens and to abuse women. Thirdly, over the past two decades Pakistan has been open not only to refugees from neighbouring countries but also to indigent workers and slave-traders. Destitute women among refugees and illegal migrants have replaced the traditional channels of flesh trade.

No government in Pakistan has shown a commitment to women's rights for the simple reason that women's deprivation or their sexual exploitation is not an issue or their survival. Their neglect of women does not prevent them from coming to power nor does it become a factor of their ouster from office. The utmost the governments in Pakistan have done is to create commissions; of inquiry. There have been three in the last 26 years alone. The fact that the Bhutto government in the seventies, the Zia regime in the eighties, and the present government have equally resolutely disregarded the recommendations of the commissions set up by them clearly reflects only their lack of commitment. This lack of commitment and sincerity is the most serious issue in Pakistan today.

It is difficult to say anything about the methods that have worked. The main areas of difficulties are inadequacies in legislation to protect women against sexual exploitation, treatment of exploited women as criminals or as accessories to their own abuse, and the increased freedom to conservative religious elements to target women.

If the State sincerely implements the recommendations of the Women's Commission at least the situation will begin to change. Some of these recommendations are:

1. Legislation should be enacted making it mandatory for all employers to respond to and monitor incidents of harassment of women at workplace.
2. Child sexual abuse should be clearly defined and harsher penalties introduced in law.
3. Trafficked women and prostitutes should be recognised as victims of a depraved society, not as criminals; serious efforts should be made to rehabilitate them.
4. Agreements should be reached with different countries to share repatriation costs of the trafficked women.
5. The punishment for sexual harassment should be enhanced to rigorous imprisonment up to 5 years. The law should be expanded so as to cover harassment with the help of written material, photographs and all forms of vulgar displays.
6. The law on rape should be rationalised. Hudood laws must be repealed.
7. The law on procurement of minor girls and on import of girls from a foreign country should be amended to include all sexual offences as punishable and should be made applicable to women of all ages.

All SAARC Member States Should Resolve That:

- The prostitutes should no longer be treated as criminals or as objects of shocking sexual abuse. They are victims of circumstances and hence should be treated as human beings like others so as to bring them into the mainstream of the social order without any attached stigma. Under no circumstance should they continue to be in the trap of flesh trade for commercial exploitation. They need to be treated with humanity and compassion so as to integrate them into the social mainstream. To achieve it, there needs to be more effective anti-poverty measures, improved flow of information, universal access to education and an equitable socialization process to counter exploitation and discrimination.

- Networking and the broadening of anti-crime measures to counter child prostitution should be promoted. All countries already have laws which can be used to protect children from exploitation. They require more effective enforcement.

- As reliance upon traditional law enforcers, such as police and inspectors, will never be adequate, community participation needs to be maximized.

- In many countries, there is a lack of authentic data. More studies must be undertaken to fill the information gap.

- There is also a lack of transit shelters and temporary home for the victims of trafficking. More resources need to be allocated to provide shelter as well as social, medical and psychological care for the victims.

- Governments must be made aware of the situation through NGO activists, journalists, parliamentarians and different segments of the society. Both the sending and receiving countries must make efforts to organize themselves to deal with this issue.

- Awareness-raising programmes must be organized at the national and regional levels through mass media, NGOs, human rights groups and community organizations.

- Governments must ratify as well as enforce international conventions on trafficking. There is also a great necessity for amending existing legislations. Legislative measures need to be strengthened to detect and punish middlemen, agents, brothel-owners, pimps and others involved in prostitution.

- To arrive at the 'Priority Objective' of zero level, both positive and negative methodologies must be adopted. Positive methods involve rescue operations and rehabilitation measures for victims already in the profession. Negative measures aim at negating entry to new entrants to the profession. For this, every country should have access to fully developed intelligence network with efficient networking of information among countries of the region.

In India, we are planning to have under our agencies an organisation based on the pattern of the Narcotics Control Bureau, (proposal for this is under formulation), for an effective information system. This will be a nodal agency which will have representatives from all law enforcement agencies like the Central Bureau of Investigation, Central Police Force, Border Security Force, representatives from the judiciary, the Central Excise Department, NGOs and the National Commission for Women. The body will research, analyse, disseminate information and plan immediate steps for total eradication of trafficking. With this kind of agency we hope to cut across barriers and impediments of protocol and bureaucracy which have slowed down all past measures to stamp out the malaise of child prostitution.

In retrospect thinking together we can move forward. Ideas don't need any legs to stride but they need institutions to translate all the promises to real life. Likewise, cooperation must emerge. We must all cooperate to free women and children from the deplorable human rights violations being perpetrated on them.

10

Role of the National Commission for Women

In India, the question of child abuse and sexual exploitation of children has been under active consideration of the National Commission for Women (NCW), India since 1995.

The National Commission for Women is an apex body in India created by an Act of Parliament called the National Commission for Women Act, 1990 (No. 20 of 1990). The Act came into force in January, 1992. The Commission consist of a Chairperson, five members and one Member Secretary—all nominated by the Central Government. The main functions of Commission are to investigate and examine all matters related to the safeguards provided for women under the Constitution and other laws; to forward recommendations for the effective implementation of those safeguards for improving the conditions of women by the Union or and State; to take up the cases of violation of the provisions of the Constitution and of other laws relating to women with the appropriate authorities; to look into complaints and take *suo motu* notice of matters relating to either deprivation of women's rights or non-implementation of laws enacted to provide protection to women or non compliance of policy decisions and to take up such matters with appropriate authorities; to call for special studies or investigations into specific problems or situations concerning women and thereby recommend strategies for their removal; to inspect or cause to be inspected a jail, remand home, women's institution or other places of custody where women are kept as prisoners or otherwise, and take up with the concerned authorities for remedial action, if found necessary; to fund litigation involving issues affecting a large body of women.

All the reports need to be laid before each House of Parliament along with memorandum explaining the action taken or proposed to be taken on the recommendations. The Commission also has all the powers of a Civil Court trying a suit and in particular in respect of the matters namely—summoning and enforcing the attendance of any person from any part of India and to examine him on oath; requiring the discovery and production of any document; receiving evidence on affidavits; requesting any public record or copy thereof from any court or office to issue to the Commission for the examination of witnesses and documents and any other matter which may be prescribed.

Keeping in mind the fact that commercial exploitation of children and traffic in persons for commercial sex abuse is the worst form of violation of human rights, and the number of children entering the trade is on the increase, sexual exploitation of women and children became a key area of concern for the Commission. In view of it, studies were commissioned in ten States to assess the magnitude of the problem. The findings of the studies revealed a very dismal and horrible position.

In order to focus attention on the problem, the Commission organized conferences, workshops, debates and meets during 1995. The Chairperson and Members of NCW made a nationwide tour and met more than 80,000 women in prostitution and child prostitutes in different States of India, got acquainted with their problems, environmental conditions, health status, their requirements and concerns. The Commission held several consultations with NGOs and activists. NCW also sponsored research studies in the States of Orissa, Goa, Andhra Pradesh, Kerala, Karnataka, Rajasthan, Delhi, West Bengal and a part of Madhya Pradesh which includes survey of several brothels and streets in order to get firsthand authentic information regarding the status of child prostitutes.

The studies revealed a dismal position and confirmed the apprehensions of NCW that the network involves not only traffickers but pimps and brothelkeepers also who work in connivance with the police. Alarmed by the situation, the NCW, organised a National Consultation on Sexual Exploitation of Children in Goa on 23-24th July, 1997 which made several recommendations for the rescue and rehabilitation of prostitutes and prevention of entry of new girls into the profession. The recommendations have been sent to the concerned Departments of Government of India and all the State Governments for follow-up action. The State Governments are taking effective and prompt action on the recommendations of NCW with a view to eliminating the evil. The NGOs are being more actively involved.

The Commission has been resolutely striving to improve the condition of women and usher a new culture by trying to eliminate gender discrimination. In pursuance of its goals, the Commission has constituted several Expert Committees to look into specific issues relating to women and give their recommendation for further action. The NCW had also defined its priorities and thrust areas and has initiated several plans and programmes to implement them. The thrust areas of NCW include: *speedy justice for women* through Parivarik Mahila Lok Adalats, *legal awareness programmes* for Women's Colleges by providing legal training to teachers and students to spread massive legal awareness; *custodial justice*—in coordination with National Human Rights Commission trying to implement support and *rehabilitation measures for women undertrials and prisoners, widows, destitutes and recommend to government for rehabilitating women and children in prostitution* and women in mental asylums, by establishing network with NGOs, State Commissioners for Women, Minorities Commission, Law Commission, University Women's Study Centre, UN and other international agencies and State Coordinators, *anti-arrack campaigns, political empowerment of women,* creating awareness and empowering women *of Scheduled Castes and Scheduled Tribes, Sathins, grass roots workers* and also *economic empowerment* of women through *transfer of technology.*

The NCW has successfully handled critical issues of atrocities on women, e.g., the Uttarkhand, incident outraging modesty of women, sexual harassment at work, dowry harassment and death and gender based denial of opportunities. In order to achieve its goals, I travelled widely all over India, held consultations with women in remote villages and had meetings with women of every section. To create awareness among the public several seminars and meetings had been held from time to time, the proceedings of which are carefully recorded to formulate plans of action. During such visits the plight of women and especially of young girls of a tender age of ten years selling out their bodies for two rupees was observed by me as the Chairperson. They are either pushed into this practice by parents due to poverty or are victims of trafficking.

The Government of India as also most of the State Governments. are aware of the enormity of the problem of child prostitution. Under the orders of the apex court of the country a Central Committee under the Department of Women and Child Development has been formed which is looking into the different aspects of the problem. There is also a proposal to convene a meeting of SAARC countries to finalize SAARC regional convention of combatting trafficking in women and children in the region.

To prevent entry of children in prostitution, NCW has involved the prostitutes themselves to undertake this onerous responsibility. The women themselves came forward and declared that they will be able to prevent it and assured me as Chairperson that entry of children into this profession would be tackled. They were also ready to inform new child entries to the NCW or the State Commissions instead of the police.

Braving the mafia and its criminal nexus the women and children in prostitution offered to undertake this responsibility which is not only laudable but most welcome. The NCW firmly believes that this will be a feasible modality to save children from prostitution. While rehabilitation has to encounter numerous hurdles and handicaps preventive measures are thought of as urgently needed and a practical solution.

During my visits to various States it has become a part of regular agenda for the Commission to have meetings with the women in prostitution, with a view to find out the difficulties being faced by them and their children and also to chalk out action plans for amelioration of their problems.

Women have come forward to seek adequate shelter for themselves and their children. They also express their willingness to opt out of this demeaning profession if they are provided shelter and a modest income of Rs. 1,000-1,500 per month. I have appreciated the reality of such women who came forward in large numbers to lead a normal life away from exploitation and dishonour. Their immediate need for shelter, skill, employment and regular income can no longer be over looked and demands the immediate attention of government and public.

The goal of NCW is to achieve "zero level" child prostitution. To achieve this, the Commission is formulating a ten-year National Plan of Action (1997-2006 A.D.). Split into two parts, the plan would coordinate with the Ninth and Tenth Five-Year Plans of India.

To arrive at the 'priority objective' of zero level, the Commission intends utilizing both positive and negative methodologies. Positive methods involve rescue operations and rehabilitation measures for victims already in the profession. Negative measures aim at negating entry to new entrants to the profession. For this, the Commission intends to have access to fully developed intelligence network. There have been significant advances in meeting the problem head on over the past three years. Awareness raising and public information campaign on children's issues have been pursued with vigour. There is a strong NGO movement in India. They are in the forefront of the crusade against child abuse and commercial sexual exploitation. The National Commission for Women recognizes their contribution in responding to the needs of the children as well as their advocacy efforts on the issues both at the local and international fronts. Thus, it is imperative that all concerned—the government, NGOs, the media and the community pay more attention to strengthen response mechanism; to reorient cultural attitudes and social values to be more sensitive to the child; to increase advocacy for children's right, and to work towards a more active participation of children in all matters affecting their lives.

11

Interaction with Buds

Nepal

Saroj

She was merely nine years old, content with her daily work, play and the scolding she frequently received. Her father sold her to "the Bombay man" for $14. That man asked her if she would like to go to India's entertainment capital. She remembers thinking: "Bombay is where all the films come from" and excitedly agreed.

Her first stop, though was at Bordello in the northern Indian border town of Gorakhpur, where she was "broken in" as she says. Then Saroj was sent to Pila House, one of Mumbai most decadent brothels. She was put in a small room with a tiny window that had iron bars on it. On one wall there was a calendar that had a picture of the mountains and she was reminded of her house with mountains.

For fifteen days she was beaten and whipped until she agreed to service clients. At 3 p.m. everyday she was forced to put on make-up and wait. On average she serviced six men a day for Rs. 60 ($1.60) a session. She never saw any money for five years, until her employer's investment was paid off. Saroj says she was constantly ill but could only visit a local medical quack with an escort for 10 minutes at a time.

Now seventeen and a bonded prostitute, she lines the dim, beaten stained corridors of Pila House night after night along with other girls, their faces eerily beautiful as though airbrushed for a pornographic magazine. "I send my family in Nepal Rs. 1000 [$27] per month," she says. "Sometimes I also send them video cassettes of myself with messages. We have a lot of countrymen who charge a small sum to take money and messages to my family. "Saroj has not been back to her village near Kathmandu since she left nor does she plan to return. "What will I do there?" is her query.

Mumbai has given her a two-year old son, and tuberculosis! and has also tested HIV positive! "I don't care if I die but I would like my son grow up somewhere else" she says wistfully. The toddler sleeps under her bed while she services clients. Does she insist on condoms? "No. If I talk about condoms, the client wants to know if I have a disease. I have no bargaining power." The Gharwali (brothelkeeper) has promised her a ticket home if she gets worse. "I will just be a liability and of no use to anyone if my body deteriorates" she says matter-of-factly.

A visit to Saroj's village in the Sindhupalchowk district of Nepal on a hot afternoon showed that her house was one of the few with a corrugated-tin roof and a radio. Her brother was playing cards at a nearby tea shop and her father was sleeping. Her mother was working on someone else's field. Saroj's brother and those hanging out with him were resentful of questions. "What is the harm?" he asks, referring to his sister working as a prostitute in Mumbai. "At least she can contribute to her family. Our neighbour's daughter has just come back [from India] after 18 years. She has brought back Rs. 25,000($680) cash and 12 tolas (140g) of gold." — Brother's love and father's greed. Nepal has become one of the most accessible areas for sex traffickers working in South and West Asia.

Reema

She was barely twelve when a smooth-talking flesh trader lured her to Mumbai from Kathmandu. The starry-eyed girl wanted to become a film actress. Instead, she was sold to a brothel. At first she resisted—screaming, crying and attacking all prospective customers. But the madam who ran the brothel would have none of it. She sent in a muscled tough to pin the girl down while an old man deflowered her. The pain was so intense that Reema lost consciousness and had to be hospitalised for a week. After that it was back to the brothel. There, other child prostitutes told her she could not win this one-sided battle.

But Reema's spirit was not broken. Nine months later she

escaped from the brothel and got into a Howrah-bound train, hoping to eventually reach her home in Nepal. At Howrah, a soft-spoken lady promised to help; she lured the young girl to a Calcutta brothel and sold her. Reema had only managed to escape from one brothel to another.

Now, Reema appears resigned to her fate. She hits the streets of central Calcutta as soon as it gets dark and stands under a lamp-post soliciting customers. Her parents in Nepal have no idea where their daughter is. She does not have the courage to tell them the truth and cannot make herself lie; and anyway, they probably think that she is dead and it is better that way, she insists. But she still dreams of making enough money to escape to a life of freedom and dignity.

Mira

Mira was thirteen years old when a man from Mumbai came to her remote village in Nepal looking for a domestic servant. He was offering 600 rupees a month, a fortune to subsistence farmers scratching out a living. Mira wanted to go. Not only had Mira never gone to school but she had never ventured beyond her village. She imagined Mumabi would be a magical place filled with Hindi movie stars. She knew that if she stayed at home she would become a burden to her father who couldn't afford to pay the dowry for her marriage.

Mira was bundled off in a produce truck which took her to Mumbai. She quickly realised she would not be working as a domestic servant at all. She was delivered to a brothel in the notorious Falkland Road, where tens of thousands of women and girls are displayed in row after row of cages. Mira was locked into a narrow windowless room without food or water. On the fourth day, when she still refused to work, one of the brothel-owner's thugs banged her head against the concrete floor until she passed out. She was raped, made-up with cheap cosmetics and forced to entertain clients.

The brothelowner told her that she had been sold to the brothel for 50,000 rupees and that she had to work to pay off the debt. She was never allowed to leave the red-light area and, in any case, where would she go? In Mira's case, her freedom from the brothel was purchased by a client who became her pimp. Today, at the age of 35, no longer prostitute, she runs a small tea shop in Mumbai. (Extract from "India's Shame," published by *The Nation*, 8th April, 1996.)

Delhi

Urmila

Urmila is tall, lean and dark in complexion and 15 years old. She lost her father at the age of ten; she has two younger sisters. Her mother is running charcoal business and her monthly income is only R.150/- Within this meagre income she has to run the family. At the age of 12 she was fond of seeing cinemas; but she was not permitted to see any films by her mother. One day for the first time she went to see a movie evening show (6 p.m. to 9-30p.m.) without informing her mother. She was afraid that her mother would beat her severely for late coming, so she wanted to stay outside. She saw some young girls sleeping on the door steps of the shops in the vegetable market; she also slept along with other girls. The next morning, she could see the young girls selling vegetables and making money; so she also started selling vegetables. She could see more and more films with the money she earned. Besides, it was an added income to the family; her mother also encouraged her mean while she could see some of her friends spending money lavishly. She learnt that other vegetable vendors used to have illicit relationship with rickshawalas who bring vegetables to the shops. Soon Urmila was also in the trap. When her mother knew what the girl was up to she chained and kept her in the house. One day, she ran away and landed up in a brothel.

Tamil Nadu

Radha

Fifteen-year old Radha is short statured and looks neither attractive nor ugly. Her father is a mat seller at Tiruchendur and was earning sufficient income. He was having a concubine and lived with her. Her mother had deserted him because of his ill-treatment. Owing to the ill-treatment of the step-mother, Radha came to her sister's house and stayed with her for six months. Her brother-in-law misbehaved with her during her stay; she reported the matter to her sister; her sister quarrelled with her husband and then asked her to stay in her father's house. By that time she was ten years old, she came to the bus stand and started begging to get some cash for travel. Meanwhile, she came across an old lady, who took her to a house where there were seven young girls who smoked, drank and played cards. It was a brothel. She was forced into prostitution. So she ran away and came to her father's house. After some days father, step-mother and brother came to know about her stay at the brothel and drove her away from the house. So she was left in the streets. Meanwhile, Radha passed from girlhood to womanhood. She planned to visit her aunt's house at Tirunelveli. While she was begging at the bus stand, she met a teenaged girl who took her to another brothel.

Rosa

Rosa is an eighteen -year old mother. She is short, fat and wheat yellowish in complexion. She hails from Thalaikulam village of Kanyakumari district. Her father, a radio mechanic earns a measly income of one hundred rupees. Her mother is a casual coolie and her income is uncertain on most days. Rosa is the second child to her parents, her elder brother is an agricultural labourer and the younger two sisters are studying in seventh and fifth standards respectively. She went to school up to the fourth standard and thereafter she was make to look after household affairs. She was given in marriage, to a jobless man, who went to Thiruvanantha puram in search of a job. He never returned and thus she was deserted. Meanwhile she delivered a male baby too. She felt that both her child and herself are incumbent on her parents. Often she ran into conflict with her parents over financial matters. One day her son became sick and she wanted to take him to the Government Hospital at Kottar, Nagarcoil, so she sought the help of her mother for the bus fare and other expenses. Her mother refused to give the money, instead told her to give the child locally available native medicine. But she borrowed money from the neighbours and came to the hospital. After taking the treatment for her son, she was not having money to go to Thalaikulam. At the hospital she met one middle-aged lady, who told her that she would offer her a job and took her to a house located in Kulathankarai in Nagarcoil (otherwise known as the red-light area of Nagarcoil). She found there were young girls making money through the flesh trade. As she was deserted by her husband, and left with no means of subsistence, she volunteered to enter into this easy profession to maintain her livelihood.

Rajammal

Rajammal is a beautiful, tall and fair complexioned girl with lovely long hair. She belongs to Narasinganallur village in Tirunelveli district. She is seventeen years old. Her father is a physically handicapped person and can't walk properly. He is running a petty shop. The mother is a beedi worker. She is the eldest child to her parents; other youngsters are three brothers and four sisters. She often went to the cinema without the permission of her parents and was an uncontrollable child. She developed friendship with a rickshawala at the age of sixteen. Both loved each other. This news reached the ears of her parents; they often used to beat her whenever she went outside the house without permission. One day her lover took her to cinema for the evening show. After seeing the cinema he told her to come along with him to Tuticorin, where they can get married and settle. Believing all these sweet words, she went along with him to Tuticorin. At Tuticorin, both were staying in a house known to her lover. A few days later he told her that he was going to Tirunelveli and he would return back within two days. But he never returned. Later, she came to know that the house lady was a brothelkeeper and that she had been sold for Rs. 500. In this manner she was forced into prostitution. She refused and ran away to Tirunelveli in search of her husband. She could not trace him out in the big city. She was wandering here and there to the bus stand; meanwhile she was caught by the police under suspicion and was kept in the police custody. She was released on bail with the help of an old lady. Thereafter she was engaged in beedi making in the old lady's house. Unfortunately one day, the policeman who caught her the previous time came that side. As he wanted a case for that day, without any reason he caught her and charged her. She was again released after a few days. These situations frustrated her and she went again voluntarily to the brothel house at Tuticorin.

Susheela

Susheela hails from Madhuranthangam and is fifteen years old.

She had studied till 9th class, but does not have any skills that will find her a job. She was forced to agree to marry a man much older than her. Three days later she came of age, and decided to leave home before the wedding with the help of a young man who worked in the local tea shop. After her arrival in Chennai she lived with this young man for four months. Then he left her with no money, clothes, shelter or food. Although she had an aunt in Chennai she did not wish to contact her because she would send her back to the village.

While wandering around the city she met up with a brothelowner who took her home. Later she was asked to get dressed and entertain men. She later got used to it. Since then she had been sold twice to different brothels. She finally escaped and attempted to make a living by selling flowers and fruits with the help of some friends. This had been difficult as she had no capital. She still has no shelter and sleeps on railway stations or platforms. Hunger continues to drive her to prostitution. She wishes to have at least a place to sleep.

West Bengal

Sadhna

Fourteen-year old Sadhna lived in a village of central Bengal and dreamt of visiting Shantiniketan and Calcutta. A friend offered to take her to these places. But instead of a pilgrimage to Rabindranath Tagore's abode of peace Sadhna was taken to Sonagachi, Calcutta's biggest red-light area where about 50,000 prostitutes live. There, she was brutally raped and told she would be killed if she did not entertain customers. She did not have the courage to fight back. Then onwards, hers has been a dark world.

Three years have passed since then. Now Sadhna considers herself lucky if she gets customers who pay her not for sex — which she hates but just to talk. They pay Rs.30/- just to sit beside her, and perhaps hold her hands. Last fortnight, she got one such customer. She told him that she likes Hindi songs and has recently acquired a tape recorder. She drinks often as it helps her forget her throubles temporarily.

She hears that her customer has come to Sonagachi in a blue

Maruti and wants to go for a ride. The customer, who discovers that Sadhna has never seen any part of Calcutta except Sonagachi, agrees. As the car speeds through Calcutta, Sadhna is transported into another world. She exclaims that it is the best day of her life.

But when the car turns back towards Sonagachi, Sadhna is saddened and retreats into silence. By the time the car enters the filthy lanes of the red-light area, tears glimmer in her eyes. Still, she steadies herself and with a plastic smile, bids her customer good bye. Sadhna knows there is no escape from her sordid world.

Shova Sasmal

Shova Sasmal is nineteen years old and comes from a very poor family. She was forced into prostitution by a relative rather a neighbour. She was sold into a Mumbai brothel and worked for about three years there. She was rescued by the police in 1995 and was kept in Liluah Home. Sanlaap appealed for her custody. Soon she was sent to Sanlaap shelter and was living with 22 other children. When it was found out that Shova is also HIV positive, counselling and motivation programmes were taken up. She is a brave girl who accepted her sickness with a smiling face.

The village chief and other villagers have decided to pay her a small amount (Rs.15000/-) from the woman who took her to Calcutta, and the woman has agreed to give it. This trafficker woman has told us that she only trafficked Shova to Calcutta and another man took her to a Mumbai brothel. The name of this man is Gopal Singh and he works at Fairlie Place (Railway) in the personal department. Sanlaap with the help of Panchayat Pradhan could have turned this woman to the police - and gone to the court but there is no substantial or concrete evidence as proof. The trafficker will invariably be out on bail before long and the case can go on for twenty years. By that time Shova might even succumb to death of AIDS.

Andhra Pradesh

Kamala

Kamala is thirty-two years old, born in Dommari caste and lives in Tadepalligudem. Dommari is a caste which practises prostitution as a caste profession. Kamala grew up as a child with lots of play and the freedom of a child. She never went to school. She was unaware of her mother's profession. She attained puberty at the age of ten years. Thereafter her mother curbed her movements of play and started dressing her like a woman. She was exhibited often to strange men. Whenever she come across strange men in her house she used to be terribly scared. She knows her neighbour, a young man who used to behave intimately with her. She trusted him as a brother. She used to share with him her fear of strange men and her mother's strong control. He became very intimate to her and assured that she will be liberated by him from her house. He promised to marry her and live with her. He lured her with number of promises. One night Kamala left her house along with him. Both of them reached Machalipatnam the next morning. After ane day's stay and visit to the movies at Machalipatnam he brought her to Tirupati saying that he was going to marry her there. There, she was shocked to see the other side of his face. Suddenly, he became aggressive, threatened her with abusive language and assaulted her sexually. Even before she could recover from the shock, she was already sold for Rs. 5000/- to another person. He took her by force and confined her to a hut in the slums of Tirupati and made her starve. She tried to escape but failed because of vigilant pimps. Her escape bid resulted in further torture and injuries being inflited upon her. The neighbourly women and an elderly women comforted her but slowly initiated her into prostitution. She lived under the iron hand of the man and submitted herself every night to more than eight men. She had to also submit herself to frequent visitors even during daytime. She became mechanical in habit and just survived on the meagre food given to her. After about three years of her pitiable life another man purchased her and took her to Vijayawada. She remained a prostitute for four years in Vijayawada slums. Ultimately she got infected by STD. She fell sick often, but could not discontinue her profession. She hardly had money for treatment. Even the tips she received sometimes from the clients were collected back by the "Aunty". Unable to bear the torture and suffering she was initiated into consuming country liquor.

One morning a party of three men came to her and asked her to follow. She understood that she was further sold again. She was shifted to Chilakaluripet and asked to entertain truck drivers, cleaners and drunkards. The clients used to not only abuse her sexually but sadistically torture her physically, until she became used to it. Until then the clients were brought into her hut/house. But in Chilakaluripet she was asked to stand at the National Highway to attract customers. That is how the responsibility of bringing customers fell on her. She spent another years at Chilakaluripet where she was not even fed properly. Her health had deteriorated vastly. Twice she had to undergo abortions; she underwent surgery. Ultimately one day the strong man asked her to get out of the place as she was no more useful, although she was only 32 years of age.

In search of her parents she reached Tadepalligudem and found that her parents had expired. Currently, she doesn't have a home. Her caste people recognized her and gave her a shelter. But she has no alternative for livelihood. She stands at the roadway of Tadepalligudem and solicits customers on account starvation. She is affected with many ailments and lead a life of orphan. Her income is also meagre. Yet she shares it with others. She is a completely broken women with no future and no hope on her face. She behaves mechanically, often becoming silent on account of her misfortune and suffering.

Kalavati

Kalavati is twenty-one years old and born to Janamma. She doesn't know her father's name. She has a sister. She belongs to 'bogam' caste (dancing girls). Their profession is dancing during the marriages and festivals though she never danced. Her mother used to dance and also continues the profession of prostitution. She takes good care of her two daughters who are her hopes in continuing the business. Kalavati is an attractive girl who attained puberty at the age of twelve. Attracted to her personality a Marwadi middle-aged man paid Rs. 75,000 in instalments and took her to Mumbai and kept her as his mistress. She was kept in an apartment in Mumbai. Besides the Marwadi person she was also introduced to three-four other men and coaxed to satisfy them. While she lived as the mistress of the Marwadi man, he encouraged her to earn some more money by providing sex service to a select few brought by him. She was in Mumbai for four years. The Marwadi man brought her back home and left her with her mother.

The Marwadi is a businessman and visits her once a month. Her mother has now stopped the profession and maintains Kalavati and her sister in the profession but for only selected clients. Kalavati is a careful girl, she owns a house and demonstrates the Mumbai life style. Therefore, she is in great demand but she is very choosy. She told us that she is very happy and doesn't want to leave the profession. Kalavati is the rare example being well-off in the profession but still such people are there.

GOA

Manjula

Manjula, is a young nine year old minor girl lived with her maternal uncle and aunt in Caraswado, Mapusa. She would come every morning around 9 a.m. to sell plastic bags. In the afternoon she would spend some time in the open school. After that she would continue selling plastic bags till about 7 p.m.

Manjula would be very badly dressed and did not possess even a pair of slippers. She would earn only Rs.30/- per day and this would be given to her uncle. She would eat only one frugal meal in the morning ; the rest of the day she would survive on cheap snacks available in the market. After a period of nine months, Manjula was seen sporting a smart hair cut started and dressed well, which seemed odd. Her teacher in the open school questioned her and found out that she had about Rs. 300 in her possession.

When Manjula was questioned about it, she told that she was helping somebody to vend articles on Calangute beach. Her mannerisms had changed and she became very cautious about what she spoke. She had around Rs. 500 that day too. From that day she stopped coming to the open school. She refused to talk to the teacher and interact with the other children.

Later she was seen on the beach and her behaviour was alarming. Manjula was not the spontaneous child known for past nine months. She was very uneasy and rude due to the intrusion by others into aspects of her private hidden life. She spoke a smattering of broken English and spoke with an air of false maturity. She said she felt sick and did not like eating athough her periods had not yet started so she was afraid though whatever was meant by that was not comprehensible. Manjula did not want to speak to anyone in private. She sent a message that she could not come to school as she was leaving for Bijapur district.

Tanu

Tanu hailed from a well-off family in Bijapur in Karnataka and has studied up to class VII in Kannada medium in her village school. Her maternal uncle was the secretary of the Village Panchayat and held the respect of the whole village. He used to often send the Panchayat peon Sangappa to do petty errands at Tanu's house and before anybody knew what was happening Tanu eloped with Sangappa who brought her to Vasco-da-Gama in Goa, rented a house at Mangor Hill and told her that they will get married once he gets a job. Eight days later Sangappa went out in search of a job and never returned home. Tanu waited for two days before approaching a neighbour. She did not have any money, nor did not know the local language and did not know anybody. She was just thirteen years old then and was very scared. Her neighbours who were also from Karnataka refused to help her. Only the family who rented her the room being local fisherfolk asked her to work in the house to repay their rent. The lady of the house gave her leftover food and asked her to do all the housework. Trouble started two days later, when late in the night the lady's husband forced himself upon Tanu. He told her he would kill her if she told anybody about it. This continued for a week till she dreaded the approaching nights. One night she just walked out on the road and got lost. A man casually spoke to her in her own language and asked for her service for money which she agreed. Two days later she was with Jhansi amma—her gharwali. After a fortnight the red-light area was raided and Tanu found herself in jail. Within a brief period of two months the whole course of her life had changed just because she was foolish enough to elope. That was seven years back, recalls Tanu with tears rolling down her cheeks. Within these seven years she has had four abortions, and also has a son who is three years old. Tanu has also recently bought a room measwing 5×2 mts for herself which cost her Rs. 28,000. It has no municipal tax and is illegal, but so are all houses in Baina. After seven years Tanu went home to her native village. Her parents were happy to see her and although many questions were asked but she was prepared for them. Her parents believe she works as a construction worker in Goa. Sangappa is married and has three daughters. She hopes nobody treats them the way Sangappa treated her. Tanu has since the last seven months left prostitution. She works for an NGO, which looks after children of prostitutes. She helps in organising many health camps and AIDS awareness campaigns and advocates the use of condom and imparts peer education.

Malti, Soni, Durga

The first three girls were all fifteen years old. Malti, Soni and Durga, (names withheld) all came from Andhra Pradesh from the village of Hospet. Malti and Durga come from very poor families whose parents are farmers. Their gharwali Jhansi who hails from their native place in Andhra Pradesh is a respected woman in her hometown who boasts that she has "Business in Goa". She requested Malti's and Durga's parents to allow her to take them to Goa to work as housemaids, clothes, food, plus payment would be made. They would be happy and the family would have one mouth less to feed. Their families were given Rs. 2000 each with a promise to send Rs. 500 every month which was two years back. Little did Durga and Malti know what was in store for them.

For the first three days they were kept locked inside a room and were only let out for ablutions and to eat food. When they asked for work the other girls in the room first laughed at them saying they would get plenty of work. After exactly five days "Jhansi Masi" came in with two men. "We were asked her to go with the men in a Maruti car. We asked her where to go, she said don't get scared, these men will take you to work, see that you work nicely, you must make people happy then only they pay us". Malti recalls how scared she was, Durga and she both clutching each other's hands in fright, and had a premonition something bad was going to happen but they did not know what. The white Maruti car had a driver, one man sat in front and one at the back with Malti and Durga. They don't recall how long they travelled because the whole way they were pawed and pressed by the man sitting with them. Malti and Durga knew no other language other then Telugu and were at a loss what the men were talking but by their lewd behaviour and gestures they were both terribly frightened.

They related that they were taken to a hotel where they were handed over by these men to the "Sahib" waiting in the room. Durga was taken to another "Sahib" . They were made to do the most pervert acts by these men but Malti says her "Sahib" was much better. After they came back the hapless girls enquired from each other how much it pained and how many times the "Sahib" asked them to do the horrible acts "sign language". They stayed in the room for nearly six hours. That is what Malti says but Durga says that it was more. Ultimately, they were sent back because Durga was bleeding profusely.

When she was brought back on seeing her condition Jhansi Masi was furious with the men and took money from them. Durga was taken to the hospital where she was examined by a doctor who gave her an injection and medicines, which the gharwali gave her regularly. In spite of their refusals Jhansi Masi who told them to call her "Amma" coaxed them to go with men. Says Malti "We were once taken on the ship, and were so scared. We stayed with the phirangis (foreigners) the whole night. I don't know how many times we were forced to do it" and there were so many "phirangis" in the morning we could not even move our legs. But the phirangis gave us lots of things. One even gave a watch to Durga. She forgot her pain in the excitement of getting so many things—that also "Phoren". "Now we are used to it. Amma gives us good food and we are able to send around Rs. 2000 home to our family every month".

They do not want to get married and settle down. "Yes, after another two years I will go back to my village and get married but if I have daughter I will never send her to work with any masi". That was the deep sighed cry of both Malti and Durga.

Karnataka

Lakshmi

Lakshmi's grandmother was a professional person in prostitution in an area where several generations of women have been involved in this activity. Though her mother was not involved in prostitution she became involved. She had been to school till the 5th standard. Due to economical problems at home her grandmother introduced her to the profession. She had seven siblings. She had liking for this kind of earning. She had great difficulty when she initially started work. The first day was torture. She spent most of the time crying. She protested to her grandmother several times and offered to do house work but she did not listen.

There are increasing police raids nowadays and to pay fines, she had to see many more customers. It is a vicious cycle. If the police leave her alone, maybe she can save some money and then try doing something else. But right now she had no solution to her problems.

Kerala

Ramla

Ramla belonged to a middle class Muslim family in the village of Kundungal. She is the daughter of an Arabi. She has her mother and three brothers. One brother is employed in the Middle East. Her Bappa used to visit them once in two years. She could study up to VI standard, but does not know writing and reading. She cherishes her childhood memories. Bappa was very affectionate. All the members in the family had concern for her and loved her. At the age of 15, she fell in love with Rashid a man living in the neighbourhood. On the assurance of marriage from Rashid, she left home with him. Rashid brought her to Bangladesh colony. She did not know that Rashid was an alcoholic and a drug addict. Rashid could not live without drugs. When there was shortage of money Rashid began to disturb her, even physically. She had to share her bed with strangers brought by her husband, Rashid. She had no other way but to obey Rashid.

Now she goes to work on her own. She goes to the town on almost all days. Her customers are mostly business people from lodges in this town. She earns about Rs. 300 a day. Occasionally, the police arrest her and lock her up in jail for a few days.

One day Rashid disappeared suddenly. She did not get any information about him for quite a long period. Now Ramla stays with an autorickshaw driver. She has two children from this relationship. He too exploited her and made money from her work. He also deserted Ramla and married another woman. Ramla continues to do the same work even today.

Orissa

Sandhya

Sandhya, a resident of Paradeep is in a lucrative profession. She has been providing sexual services since she was fourteen years only. Her base of operation is with her mother who is a commercial sex worker. She pimps for sexual services with the assistance of three Dalals/agents named Ramu, Raju and Kaka. At fourteen she has not reached puberty and yet has been a prostitute in Paradeep for two years. She entertains at least 4/5 clients per day, though she gets lot of offers per day as she is a child prostitute. She earns Rs. 300 per day. She spent 50 per cent of her earning on food and clothes.

She has an interest to marry a boy who will love her and protect her. She is not ready to leave the profession unless she is given food and shelter and marriage partner. Her health status is not so good as she does not sleep day and night. She does not use condom as condom is not allowed by the clients.

12

Who Cares About Human Rights Issues

There are no real advocates for children. There is no community outrage when children are sleeping on the floor, under sinks and toilets or that kids are locked up with no staff or kids are abducted, sold and abused; there is no outcry

BETTY MERLER

Pandit Jawaharlal Nehru was asked by Andre' Malraux: "What has been your greatest difficulty since Independence?" and Pandit Nehru answered "Creating a just society by just means".

Indeed there are few societies which have not faced this difficulty. There has been a widely shared realisation that injecting a bill of rights into a constitution with conventional modes of judicial enforcement for some of the rights is simply not enough. The felt need to fill these glaring gaps acquired urgency as a result of shocking reports of gross human rights violations which went unredressed, such as torture and rape in police custody, custodial deaths and disappearances, ethnic and communal violence, the revival of slavery in the form of trafficking in women and bonded labour, and pervasive gender discrimination and sexual harassment.

What is meant by Human Rights?

Human rights are those rights which are basic to human survival. They are rights and obligations which flow out of our human needs. They are sometimes called fundamental rights, because they are the foundations of our humanity and must be protected.

Human rights as an expression may have a modern ring to it,

but as a concern it is as ancient as Plato and Aristotle when "humanity" literally started gaining grounds. Scholars like them taught the then rulers that people weren't subjects who are exclusively made to bow but also were "human beings" who needed to be looked after—both physically and emotionally. Leaping into modern times, there is a distant possibility that the study of human rights will become the most genuine inter-disciplinary study as it deals with humanity itself. On the practical side of it, a large number of human rights organisations have now been established all over the world to watch and protect right violation.

The human rights of women and of the girl child are an inalienable, integral and indivisible part of universal human rights. Women's place in every community is vital to the well-being of that society; for, without their work, both in the formal sector and in the family, most communities would not survive. It is now well recognised that enhancing women's status and enforcing their rights on an equal basis with men will do much to achieve the objectives of equality, development and peace adopted at the Fourth World Conference on Women held in Beijing in September, 1995 so essential for safeguarding human rights.

The progress of a nation is integrally linked with advancement of women. Mahatma Gandhi championed the cause of women and emphasised that "subjugation and exploitation of women was a product of men's teaching and women's acceptance". We have no dearth of laws. However, implementation of those laws are far from satisfactory. Hence when we talk about gender equity, children's rights and abuse of children, we will have to build up strategies of community participation to checkmate the evil forces all around.

No one cares, or wants to deal with a child prostitute or children of prostitute. There is no daycare for the children of families who come to court. Kids are short-changed everywhere because nobody wants to deal with them. This is especially true for child prostitutes. Everybody gives up on them. The schools don't want them. If the parents don't want them at home, the support facilities give up on them and the children remain unwanted.

Human rights abuses are wrong in themselves but they also fuel conflict-violence and hatred which result in undermining issues of justice, equity and equality before law.

Women in prostitution face systemic and entrenched discrimination and harassment in term of violence. Child prostitutes are denied access to schools, hospitals, and other public services. They face police brutality all the time and the persistent use of excessive force violates human rights totally. The problem of police abuse in brothels is not a new phenomenon. Today the problem of police abuse is one of the most pressing civil liberties issues. Durga from Bangalore recounted with tears in her eyes, how the police would come with eight to ten men and she was threatened with dire consequences, if she would not oblige. In the beginning when she resisted their demands the police would put red chilli powder in her vagina and torture her with electric shock. Unable to bear she had to succumb to their brutalities.

There are innumerable examples from all over the country of police raids, their undue demands for money, their attacks and their close links with the pimps.

The police often do not even write the reports and justify their rejection to file FIRs by suggesting that the complaints are fabricated. They also deny to file FIRs till such time they are paid and often suggest to these women that their complaints are frivolous and groundless. Sometimes the police say "that all over there are bigger tragedies that are happening, so what is the big issue if a child is molested or raped?". In another case where an eighteen-year-old girl who was molested and raped and beaten for three hours was asked by the police officer. "Why are you so upset, you have not lost your virginity?" Women hesitate to go to the police because it is a frustrating feeling to be treated like that. Sometimes women are called several times to the police stations and harassed. These interviews are generally several hours long and conducted with little regard for the trauma experienced by the victims. A fifteen-year-old victim of gang rape from Chennai told us that she had told her story to police officials at least twenty times. Another young woman who had been raped in Hyderabad, posed with exasperation, "I am tired of telling my story to everyone. I have told it at least ten or eleven times". Although the repeated questioning may be attributable to a lack of police training on how to conduct investigations into sexual violence, the effect of this relentless process is that many victims become intimidated and dissuaded from pursuing their complaints. According to a children's gynaecologist in Calcutta, almost all her clients who have experienced sexual violence refuse to go to the police because they are afraid of the questioning and investigation procedures: "It is very difficult for them to go through, all these procedures and all these interrogations. It is a tragedy."

Human rights violations take place due to police excesses on the children in prostitution. Effective and impartial policing is one of the most central components of human rights. During my various visits to the red-light areas I looked around (1) whether there was any need for change at all in the system; (2) how could the force become more representative; (3) whether mechanisms for accountability are sufficient; and (4) how could police take on a more normal policing attitude and function.

It was generally felt that a change in the system is definitely required as the police force is largely a male dominated institution. We should be recruiting more women and retaining them, and the male the dominated working environment has to be gradually changed. Of course, women within policing organisations face all the usual problem of working women, and also have the increased stress of working within what is essentially male-dominated institution.

However, the presence of more women in the police force would certainly improve the conditions for women in prostitution particularly in a segregated society, and one where the legitimacy of policing is challenged. In this regard thought should be given to the few essential aspects mentioned below:

Training: Having tried to secure a representative body of officers, how do we ensure that their training inculcates in them the important principles of adherence to the basic norms human rights, equality impartiality, and service?

In any democracy, it is vital to ensure that the police generally, as well as individual police officers, are accountable for their actions to the whole of society.

Legal accountability: What legal mechanisms for accountability are required to ensure that the police provide a proper service to the whole community without fear or favour are to be identified and laid down.

Democratic accountability: What are the mechanisms by which society can play an active role in designing and monitoring the kind of police service it wants?

Structure: What should we be looking for in any proposals regarding the structure of policing?

Transition: The above changes, if they are to occur, are dependent on those responsible consciously determining to leave behind the legacy of the past and to bring about fundamental change.

Training in Human Rights and Ethics

Few police forces in democratic societies fail to address issues of human rights in their formal training programmes. This is only proper since a fundamental objective of policing is to protect and defend the rights of all, to ensure equality before the law, and to do this by having as a primary goal the maintenance of the rule of law.

Community involvement in police training is not, however, a one-way process. It requires not only that the police be open to external involvement and scrutiny, but also requires the ready cooperation of the community. When, for whatever reason, there is distrust or suspicion between the police and parts of the community served, such cooperation may be difficult to establish.

Accordingly, it is not merely desirable for people to discuss and criticise policing — it is a civic responsibility to monitor closely how policing is carried out, and to ensure that it is discharged in accordance with established principles. Policing cannot be viewed in a vacuum. Policing is not only about how individual officers respond to pressure on the streets but it is about a whole array of factors.

It is impossible for even the best police service to please all the people all the time. The role of the police is to manage conflict in the interests of society as a whole. The police must act as neutral arbiters between opposing sides. By acting fairly and impartially they can hope to win support for their right to police.

As Lord Scarman has argued: "The success of policing operations depends in the last resort not upon questions of technique or professional expertise, but upon the degree of confidence felt by society in its police".

We should strongly condemn laws and official policies and practices that fail to distinguish between prostitutes and victims of forced trafficking, treating the latter as criminals rather than as persons who deserve "temporary care and maintenance" in accordance with international human rights standards. I strongly oppose laws and policies that punish women who engage in prostitution but not the men who operate and profit from prostitution rings and who patronize prostitutes: such policies are discriminatory on the basis of sex. Moreover, it is of great concern that effective law enforcement and social services for the victims are absent. Such attitudes towards prostitutes exacerbates the problem of trafficking.

International Legal Protection

Trafficking in persons and related abuses are prohibited under international human rights law. Governments are specifically obligated to take appropriate steps to eradicate forced trafficking in persons, exploitation for prostitution, slavery-like practices, forced labour, and coerced marriage.

Trafficking and Forced Prostitution

From the beginning, efforts to create human rights norms regarding trafficking have, in principle, focused on punishing traffickers rather than the victims. International human rights instruments that prohibit trafficking and exploitation of prostitution address these practices in broad terms. It is of particular concern that many state parties have failed to protect women and girls from coerced trafficking and forced prostitution, or have failed to prosecute vigorously those who commit such abuse.

The international community first denounced trafficking in persons in the 1949 Convention on the Suppression of Traffic in Persons and the Exploitation of the Prostitution of Others (the Trafficking Convention). Under the terms of this treaty, state parties "agree to punish any person who, to gratify the passions of another, procures, entices or leads away, for purposes of prostitution, another person ..." In addition, the Trafficking Convention requires state parties to sanction any person who runs or finances a brothel; in our view, law enforcement agencies should focus particularly on individuals who operate, aid or abet forced prostitution operations. States should further "adopt or maintain such measures as required ... to check the traffic in persons ... for the purposes of prostitution."

With regard to persons who have been trafficked, the convention emphasizes their protection and safe repatriation. It calls on state parties "so far as possible" to "make suitable provisions for trafficking victims' temporary care and maintenance"; to repatriate such persons "only after agreement ... with the State of destination"; and, where persons cannot pay the costs of repatriation, to bear the cost "as far as the nearest frontier". While we recognize the right of governments to make and enforce laws regulating national borders, they must distinguish between those who purposefully violate immigration laws and others who are victims of forced trafficking.

The obligation of state parties to take all appropriate measures to suppress the traffic in women was later reiterated in the 1979 Convention on the Elimination of All Forms of Discrimination Against Women (CEDAW). CEDAW does not, however, elaborate upon specific steps. Like the Trafficking Convention, CEDAW links trafficking to the exploitation of prostitution, but fails to address trafficking for other exploitative ends, such as coerced marriage and forced labour.

Although trafficking in women and girls has become a lucrative and expanding cross border trade, it routinely escapes effective national and international sanctions. Trafficking for the purposes of forced prostitution has frequently been mischaracterized by governments and human rights organizations alike as a voluntary act, presuming the women's consent, even when ample evidence is available to the contrary. Both forced prostitution and coerced marriage also have largely been dismissed as crimes perpetrated by private individuals for which States undertake no responsibility under international human rights law.

We in India have drafted a bill to be put up at the SAARC summit meeting to be held in Colombo, Sri Lanka in July, 1998. Some of the salient features of the draft convention are:

In the recently held Ninth SAARC Summit at Male in May 12-14, 1997, the Prime Minister of Bangladesh Sheikh Hasina categorically asserted that steps should be taken by all SAARC countries against trafficking in women and children. The Declaration of the Ninth SAARC Summit in its section on women in development stated, "Expressing grave concern at the trafficking of women and children within and between countries, the Heads of State of Governments pledged to coordinate their efforts and take effective measures to address this problem. They decided that existing legislation in Member-States should be strengthened and strictly enforced. This should include simplification of repatriation procedures for victims of trafficking. They also decided that the feasibility of establishing a Regional Convention on Combatting the Crime of Trafficking in Women and Children for Prostitution should be examined by the relevant Technical Committee."

The above meetings testify that there is not only the government's commitment at the international level, but also in the South Asian region which is the most vulnerable area at present.

The National Human Rights Commission is mandated to help develop a culture of human rights. Justice Malimath and Mr, Virendar Dayal have come out with specific strategies to combat trafficking in the Belgaum region of Karnataka. The National Human Rights Commission and the National Commission for Women are working with great dedication and speed for the human rights of these little "Thorn Buds".

The ultimate responsibility for implementation of human rights falls on the State and its legislative and executive machinery. The State has the unenviable, yet complex, duty to protect and promote individual and group rights as well as to arbitrate the conflicting claims to rights, against the overall requirements of the development of the society.

The Indian polity has, over time, and particularly in the post-Emergency era, thrown up four principal catalysts of human rights implementation, which have evolved new, often effective, strategies to catalyse rights implementation. They are the judiciary, the National Human Rights Commission, the National Commission for Women, the NGOs and the communication/ information media.

13

Situational Analysis: "Alive but Dead within"

After travelling the length and breadth of India it worried me that there was no proper data nor any studies available regarding child prostitution. I spoke to Mr. Ram Snehi of Morena, Dr. Mukherjee of Rajasthan, Dr. Indrani Sinha of Calcutta, Ms. Roma Debabrata and Ms. Bhamati of Delhi, Ms. Shyamala Natarajan of Chennai, Ms. Celsa of Goa and wanted to know if they had any data available on the subject. Their negative response was put up before the Expert Committee of the National Commission for Women, which decided that it would sponsor at least ten studies all over the country to have a situational analysis of the issue. All these reports were very useful to the Commission and were presented at the National Conference held at Goa.

I would like to dwell on the gist of these reports as meaningful recommendations and suggestions emerged from the Indian scenario on child prostitution and trafficking. Some of the suggestions made in those reports are worthwhile and would be useful.

Lost Childhood: Delhi

The lost childhood is first survey study of child prostitutes in Delhi. The causes of child prostitution have been pointed out mainly are as follows:

1. Large scale population influx from the countryside into cities in search of sustainable means of livelihood.
2. Loss of resource base-land, forest, etc. by tribals, dalits and others due to state sponsored projects like dams, mines, industries, power projects, etc.
3. Economic stress

For the purpose of the study Delhi was divided into nine zones. The data was collected by direct and indirect field observation, by interviews, group discussions, etc. At times researchers had to pose as clients, sales representatives, astrologers, etc. In each zone, a specific slum was selected on the basis of profile of that area, i.e., socio - economic structures and its notoriety in anti-social activities. Some Delhi based NGOs working in this field were also contacted to collect information.

A total of 1400 subjects were included in the study. The research team surveyed about 28 out of 86 kothas of G.B. Road where 2500 prostitutes stay. They assessed that almost 60 per cent of the total prostitutes are child prostitutes.

The report narrates incidents how the section of the State police, judiciary, doctors and guards, and the remand homes play their respective roles to hide the facts about child prostitutes thereby colluding as perpetuators of the crime instead of stopping it.

A close introspection revealed that Delhi's brothels and slums are flooded with girls brought from all over India. One can find girls from Mumbai, Chennai, Hyderabad, Calcutta, Varanasi, Haridwar, Rishikesh, Muzzafarpur, Bhubaneshwar, Amritsar, Ajmer and also from the neighbouring countries of Bangladesh and Nepal. Beside girls from communities practising prostitution as tradition were also involved in the trade in large numbers. Such communities are the Nut, Kanjar, Banchara, Bedia, Mahar, Matang, Sansi and Kolta.

The minor girls abducted and sold are hidden in Kotha Malkeen, houses in Laxminagar, Shakarpur, Vikaspuri and Rohini. Here these girls are subjected to a number of inhuman conditions. They are raped continuously, at times even red chilli powder and even burning cigarette butts are applied on their private parts. These girls are forcibly made to eat snake meat which supposedly serves as an aphrodisiac. Such barbaric ordeals continue till the girls give their consent for prostitution.

'Dallas' (pimps) play an important role in this trade. They have long nexus with the underworld and law enforcing agencies. They procure minor girls from different areas and run brothels in residential colonies.

The conditions inside the brothels is equally inhuman. Dozens of girls are huddled in small stinking rooms where they spit and do all kinds of things. These brothels have tehkhana, a hidden safe place between "do-chattas" where minor girls are hidden in case of raids by police or visits by social workers. These minor girls are made to lie about their age. For instance, a girl of fourteen will tell her age as twenty whereas her physical appearance will belie her claim. They are barred from divulging any information to any outsider or else they are tortured by malkeens or madams. The pro-situation prone areas visited by the research team were :

Prem Nagar Basti :

This area inhabits people from the Perna community. Earlier this community's source of livelihood was mainly through dacoity and kidnapping. But the Britishers ended this source of income and they were gradually drawn to this trade. The male members of the family act as pimps and the lady members of the house extend full cooperation to the woman engaged in prostitution. Firstly, daughters are introduced in the trade and after they are married, daughters-in-law are expected to continue the tradition. Girls from the tender age of 2-5 years are trained to become prostitutes and at 11-12 years of age they start serving clients.

Yamuna Pushta :

This area lies on the outskirts of Delhi flanking the river Yamuna and houses around 1,24,000 people in about 13,000 jhuggies. Sanjay Amar Colony is the most prone area for child prostitution. The area is inhabited mostly by low-income migrants from West Bengal, Bihar, Uttar Pradesh and Bangladesh. They work variously as rickshaw-pullers, rag pickers, kabadi-wallahs, and their womenfolk as maids. Their source of income is meagre while the family size is large. Hence, under great economic stress they are turned into pushing their girls into this trade when approached by procurers as sham bridegrooms. The girls of age group of 12-15 years are sold and purchased by procurers, locally known as dalaals.

The girls are used for the sex trade. They have even been taken to Arab countries as well where they work as ostensibly maids though at most times are actually sex slaves existing in horrible conditions of servitude. As many as approximately 1 lakh girls between the age group of 8-15 years have been sold in Pakistan from this area alone in the past 27 years.

Bhumiheen Camp (Govindpuri)

The Bhumiheen Camp is situated in South Delhi and houses around 15,000 people in 3,200 jhuggies. The people of this area are mainly migrants from Uttar Pradesh, Madhya Pradesh, Rajasthan, West Bengal, Bihar and Bangladesh. They too, work as rickshaw-pullers, rag-pickers, carpenters and maids. According to one of the Pradhans of this area pretty girls are soft targets of procurers. Other sources in the colony informed that minor girls between 10-16 years of age are much in demand in the nearby posh colonies. Many people of this area send money back home more than their income suggests. Police extort money regularly from households having minor girls. A quack informed that several unwed minor girl pregnancies are referred to nearby nursing homes. Then, some girls of the age group of 5-13 years left behind unprotected by their parents were also soft targets of child abuse.

New Seemapuri

New Seemapuri is on the eastern fringes of the capital. It houses about 28,000 people in 4,750 jhuggies. The people staying in this area originally belong to Uttar Pradesh, Madhya Pradesh, West Bengal and Bangladesh. They are mostly involved in rag-picking, rickshaw-pulling and as industrial workers, whereas the women are engaged as domestic maids in nearby posh areas.

About 60-70 minor girls are already involved in the trade and 40 per cent of minor girls fall in the highly prone category. The flesh trade is linked with drug peddling too. The kingpins of the trade are residents of this area and operate in an organised manner. The minor girls are kept in their custody and introduced as their daughters. Girls from this area are supplied to Delhi-UP border and even to Arab countries.

Nizamuddin Basti

It is situated in Central Delhi. Approximately 3000 people stay in 500 jhuggies. These people are mainly from Bihar, Maharashtra, West Bengal and Bangladesh. Menfolk of the area work as rag-pickers, rickshaw-pullers, daily wage labourers, cooks, etc. and the women either stay indoors or work as domestic maids.

Some of the girls of this Basti have been married at a very tender age and have been left behind by their husbands who stay in Arab countries and never send money back. Hence, out of economic compulsion they are driven to this trade.

Firstly, the minor girls are brought from Bangladesh, exploited sexually for days and then pushed into the trade. Night shelters and public conveniences have transformed into dens for sexual misdemeanours.

Seva Nagar

Seva Nagar is a huge Jhuggi-Jhopri cluster, housing around 22,000 people. The occupants of this area hail from Bihar, Uttar Pradesh and the southern states. Men work as rag-pickers, industrial workers and construction labourers, etc. while the women mostly stay indoors. Apparently, the research team did not find evidence of the prevalence of flesh trade.

Jahangirpuri

It is situated in the outskirts of North Delhi and is one of the biggest slum colony of metropolis. Approximately 12,000 people live in 3,000 jhuggies, who have migrated from Uttar Pradesh, Bihar, West Bengal and even Bangladesh. Majority of menfolk work as rag-pickers, rickshaw-pullers, factory labourers, vendors, etc. Women work in factories, assist their husbands or are domestic maids. The residents vehemently denied operation of flesh trade in their area.

Rohini

Rohini lies in the north-western part of the capital. The survey of three clusters-Durga Vihar, Sanjay Camp and Rajiv Camp revealed that about 6,000 people inhabit these areas. People have migrated from Rajasthan, Bihar and Uttar Pradesh.

Flesh trade is intrinsically linked with drug peddling and bootlegging carried on try the Sansi community. Local sources suggested that they work with consent of police and minor girls are supplied within and outside the colonies. The study also revealed that certain hotels and guest houses are also involved in the flesh trade where mostly minor girls are supplied to the clients.

A long list of recommendations has been given by the research team. Some of the important ones being as follows:

1. The ITPAct needs to be amended to treat child prostitution as rape hence punishable under section 412 of the Cr. P.C.
2. Grass roots bodies like panchayats, teachers, anganwadi workers should be involved for creating awareness among people and in registration of each marriage in the area.
3. Regulatory bodies like the police, judiciary, panchayats, etc need to be sensitized.
4. Integrated community development schemes and income generating schemes should be launched for the rehabilitation of child prostitutes.
5. Voluntary organisations need to be empowered so as to provide protection to the rescued children.

However, though the team was successful in carrying out the study in Delhi but not without facing problems such as:

- non-cooperation from the prostitution prone areas;
- police stations;
- non-availability of information pertaining to child prostitutes;
- child prostitutes could not be identified outside the brothel;
- voluntary organisations and persons in-charge of records were very uncooperative.

Lifeline : Orissa

A study in Orissa was carried out by Jeewan Rekha Parishad. According to the report out of ten million prostitutes all over the world about two million are children. Further, the number of girls involved in immoral trafficking is around five lakh for India and around one thousand for Orissa.

INTER-STATE FLESH TRADE

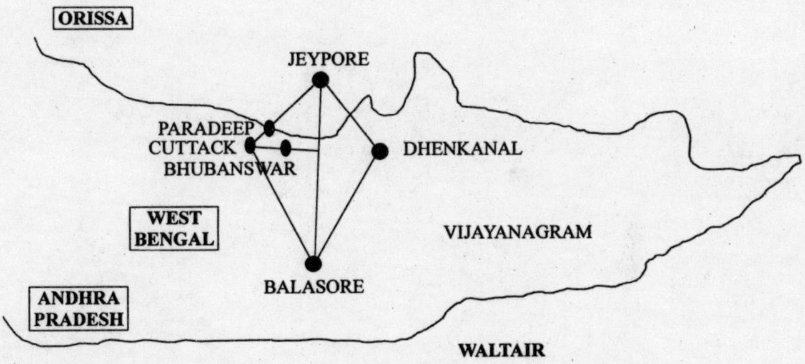

Large number of girls in Orissa are in this trade due to cultural traditions such as the Devadasi system. Inequality among various castes too plays its role among the urban, rural and tribal communities. Factors like poverty, illiteracy, ignorance and deception are not far behind in contributing their own respective reason to push these girls into the vicious circle.

Another form of sexual exploitation observed was pornographic performances and involving girls into unlawful sexual activity. The most prone areas for such activities are the drought affected and backward districts of the state such as Kalahandi and Koraput. Along the state highway passages especially in districts of Khurd and Behrampur, prostitution is rampant.

In India on the whole, demand for young prostitutes is directly related to rural-urban migration, breaking down of joint family system and increase in nuclear families, unemployment, which is currently at 17 million and a strong desire to acquire consumer goods, etc.

According to the report the incidence of STD/HIV (AIDS) are also on the rise and by the turn of this century about five million are estimated to be HIV infected. In Orissa, places like Konark, Puri, Paradeep and Bhubaneshwar are prime tourist and religious places. The tourists, both foreigners and Indians visit these places and add to the already existing demand for prostitutes.

On the one hand, the government denies any existence of child prostitution in the state while on the other newspapers and other media report that child prostitution is rampant in Orissa especially in Phulbani, Kalahandi, Balasore, Paradeep and Puri. In the absence of any proper study on child prostitution in Orissa this study was conducted.

The study was conducted in Paradeep in three phases where 100 prostitutes were contacted at random. In a structured interview, questionnaires were used to collect information in local language, i.e. Oriya.

The study revealed that 25 per cent of the total were child

prostitutes, i.e. below eighteen years while the rest were above eighteen years; 48 per cent were absolutely illiterate, while 50 per cent had attained at least primary education and 2 per cent higher secondary education or more. One interesting fact that the study revealed was that all the 100 prostitutes contacted had alternate occupations-that of vegetable vendors, maid servants, beauty parlour attendants, factory workers, daily wagers and even students.

Among the reasons for joining the profession, at the top was poverty (38 per cent), drug addiction (13 per cent), unstable marriage or desertion by spouse (12 per cent), family tradition (10 per cent), ill-treatments by parents (8 per cent), dejection (6 per cent), illness in family (5 per cent), kidnapping/abduction (4 per cent) and black mailing and religious practices (2 per cent) each.

The development of Paradeep as an industrial town has resulted in greater mobility of men alone in and out of the town, thereby creating a demand for prostitutes. This fact is supported by the type of clients who visit these prostitutes.The study reported that the prostitutes were mostly frequented by employees of industries in Paradeep (32 per cent) followed by truckers (22 per cent) and Pradeep port employee (13 per cent).

The women earn from Rs. 500 to Rs. 1000 per month after paying commissions to dalals, etc. (about 60 per cent of their total income). They spend most of the money on foodstuff, alcohol, cosmetics, dresses, etc.

Though the prostitutes included in the study were aware of the severe health problems they had been facing but still they spent very less percentage (5 per cent) on medicines. Most of them were aware of "condoms" but feared that their insistence on using it by clients may result in loss of income. Very few (26 per cent) knew what AIDS stand for and most of them (72 per cent) were ignorant about its mode of transmission. The research team found that 80 per cent of the prostitutes suffered from STDs. It was reported that truckers from Andhra Pradesh, Bihar, West Bengal were the main carriers of HIV/AIDS in Paradeep.

The children of the prostitutes were mostly less than ten years of age. They were either kept away in neighbour's, or cohabitants' house or within the premises, while carrying out their profession. However, all of them want their children to be educated, and married off at an early age. Some of the intervention measures suggested by the report are the spreading mass awareness for girls' education, preaching moral values, providing employment opportunity, the government should entrust NGOs with the welfare schemes for this infamous category of women and children and basic health care services to be provided. The report suggests rehabilitation of women and children by ensuring education, personality development and vocational training in "ashram" like schools, rehabilitative services to include counselling and medical care too. The report also suggests certain preventive-policies and programme strategies to prevent trafficking. Taxi and truck drivers should be educated on the issue, strengthening of village panchayats should be undertaken to rescue girls, NGOs should become more active, and amendment in ITPA, 1956 has also been suggested, e.g.

(i) The definition of "Public place" given in Sec 2(4) of the Act may be applicable to Sec 7(b).

(ii) The punishment provided in Sec 7 needs to be enhanced to "rigorous imprisonment" for three years and fine up to Rs. 50,000.

Some of the recommendations that emerged from the Lifeline, Orissa report are enunciated below:

1. Compulsory education to the girl child.
2. Extension of gender sensitisation and legal awareness programmes.
3. *Moral Education*: Moral education should be a part of the curriculum. Trafficking in girls is the direct result of the degradation of the moral values and norms of the society.
4. *Employment Opportunity*: Various income generation programmes should be launched to make skills available in the problem areas. If not so, other skill development trainings should be provided to women. Facilities should be provided to market their produce. Small money loans always comes in handy in the initial stages for women who

want to run any business venture.

Since traditional skills like tailoring and embroidery do not have any market now, non-traditional trainings like computer data entry, etc. be imparted.

5. *Government Intervention and Schemes for Child Prostitutes*: The following schemes of government should be implemented in the areas through NGOs:

- Short Stay Home of CSWB.
- Family Counselling Centre of CSWB.
- STEP scheme for NGOs, Ministry of Women and Children/ NORAD.
- Night Care Home by NCW.
- Thrift and credit groups of Rashtriya Mahila Kosh.
- Emergency Crisis Relief Centre (may be started by NCW).
- Homes for aged women in prostitution to minimise the spread of prostitution.
- Safe Sex Behaviour Educational Camps by NACCO, Govt. of India.
- State sponsored programmes can be implemented in collaboration with NGOs to take care of the health education and recreation of those children.
- ICDS with a compulsory adolescence girl component should be implemented in the red-light areas.

6. *Health Care Services*

- Community Based Distribution Centres (CBDS) for contraceptives should be established in the red-light areas to sell condoms under social marketing of contraceptive programmes. The CSWs should be made as CBD holders to distribute condoms.
- Condom Vending Machines developed by FPAI be installed in the red-light areas for the easy availability of condoms.
- Contraceptive promotion project be implemented by NGOs.
- Health check-up camps, blood camps etc. be conducted.
- Reproductive and sexual health camps be organised for CSWs and for their children.
- MTP (Medical Termination of Pregnancy) centre should be established in the area.

7. *Government Legislation, Laws, Police Action Courts*

- The appointment of special police officers should be notified on an emergency basis to enable the law and the associated advisory bodies to help the officers.

- Besides the police, any person or organisation authorised by the government may bring "neglected juveniles" before the Juvenile Welfare Board for treatment.
- The Central Bureau of Investigation (CBI) should be empowered to enquire and take action on trafficking in children.
- Affected areas should be regularly raided with the collaboration of NGOs.
- Courts should be given adequate authority and power to take action against powerful vested interests.

8. *Trafficking*

- Transporters like taxi and truck drivers should be educated on the issue and cooperation should be enlisted in preventing child trafficking.
- Promotion of 'family security' through the conduct of family life education and preparing the parents.
- Village Panchayats to be strengthened for rescuing the girl children in moral danger.
- The MLAs or MPs to be made accountable regarding the trafficking of girl child in their respective constituencies.
- NGOs to be encouraged for taking up effective preventive and rehabilitative supporte services.
- By recognising 'child prostitute' as "child labour in hazardous environment" the International Labour Organisation should allocate funds for taking up supportive services.
- Surveillance at border areas; inter-district; inter-State or inter-country to check child trafficking. As an incentive, awards to be declared to police or Border Security Force in instances of prevention of trafficking.

Body Imprisoned-Emotions Shackled: Karnataka

According to the report of the NCW when socio-cultural and economic conditions denies the normal upbringing of the child, the children develop socially deviant behaviour and do not adjust with their immediate environment harmoniously. Gender discrimination has many times been understood to be the root cause of the social evils like child labour and trafficking of minor girls.

It is reported that India accounts for the largest number of child prostitutes in the world (about 15 per cent) and it is increasing at a fast pace. New girls are kidnapped or bought by the middlemen and sold to the brothels. These girls mainly hail from Bihar, West Bengal, Uttar Pradesh, Maharashtra, Karnataka, Rajasthan and Nepal. According to I.L.O. 20 per cent of the total prostitutes are eighteen years of age.

The factors perpetuating child prostitution have been reported to be low female status in the family, religious factors, poverty, illiteracy, sexually abused girls, child marriage, early widowhood, abduction and unemployment. The report says that about 4,00,000 children are child prostitutes in India. The report hold tourism and HIV/AIDS pandemic for increasing demand for child prostitutes. Demand for young girls comes mainly from Asian tourists while Westerners seek young boys mostly.

The new form of prostitution that has emerged in Karnataka is the form of street girls besides the much prevalent form of Devadasi system. The child prostitutes with Devadasi background belong to districts of Belgaum, Bijapur, Gulbarga and Dharwar. Though in Bangalore prostitutes come from neighbouring states but majority of them come from Andhra Pradesh. Growing children are prone to sexual exploitation right from birth (through sale of infants), to marriages with Arabs, gang rape, etc.

The report deals with Devadasi system in detail, which has already been dealt in earlier chapters. The adverse economic conditions due to drought or severe famines pushes the young girls and women to opt for this trade. The report deals with intra and inter-State trafficking of girls. The survey was conducted of 10 girls from governmental, non-governmental homes and street-walkers. The study revealed that most of the girls belonged to Scheduled Caste or Backward classes of rural areas belonging to 16-19 years of age and had been in the profession for the past 3-5 years under economic compulsion. A few of them worked under one "Amma" who provided them food, shelter, clothing, customers and condoms as well. All the girls were aware of condoms. All had good health except one who tested for HIV. All were staying in villages and working in milk dairy and garment factories. All of them would rest in the lean periods but not all were ready to leave the profession in lieu of alternate jobs.

According to the report Karnataka has 22 observation homes, 19 juvenile homes, one special home, 8 reception centres by police, 11 state homes for women and girls and 10 shelter homes run by NGOs. A number of suggestions have been recommended in the report. Some of them are to improve the image of the girl child, to provide counselling, literacy, vocational training, etc. to the girls, stricter laws against procurers, pimps, etc. and their implementation, setting up of medical clinics in red-light area, mapping of trafficking routes; strong networking between NGOs and State Government and the grass roots workers, panchayats to be appointed as watchdogs as also sensitization of police and people about this problem.

'Unwanted Mothers': Kerala

According to this report the main reasons for prostitution are poverty, abduction, rape, Devadasi system, inter-State trafficking of women, etc. It says that in Kerala, a large majority (83 per cent) of prostitutes belong to the rural areas, especially villages surrounding three metropolitan cities, namely Thiruvananthapuram, Ernakulam and Kozhikode. The women join the profession as their husbands had deserted them, though not all were married. The women whose job becomes known to the family members are not accepted in the family. Most of them had been pregnant (94 per cent) and have one to four children normally.

The respondents had joined this profession because of childhood experience of rape, molestation, ignorance, etc. Most of them were into it because of gross economic necessity. The methodology followed to collect data was of in depth interview with four girls below eighteen years and three women in early twenties (who had been in this trade since the age of 15 years) from the Kozhikode districts residing in Bangladesh Colony and municipal corporation area. The majority of them were Muslims and natives of Kerala. All have received at least primary education. These girls practise the trade either through agents, friends or as call girls. Majority of them work when they need money or around 3-4 days a week. Their average monthly income is around Rs. 2,600-3,000 per month. Most of them are the sole bread-earners for the family and hence have no savings. They spend their money on entertainment, clothes, etc.

Some girls had run away from home due to ill-treatment, incest, deception in marriage, etc. They were not serious about their own health through none tested positive for HIV/AIDS. The respondents were into the profession by their own will but expressed their desire to leave the practice but for the sake of their children they had to continue. The report does not suggest any recommendation or rehabilitative measures.

Education without Skill : Tamil Nadu

To study the prevalence of child prostitution in the State, 11 districts and 15 towns/cities were surveyed. The data was collected by choosing at random—60 women, 14 NGOs, six brothels, four police stations and six government organisations. A separate questionnaire was designed for each group besides carrying out structured interviews.

The survey of 60 women revealed that their age group varied from under eighteen to early twenties. They have been in the profession from less than two years to more than five years. Almost all the women were from interior villages. Though 20 women opted for this trade but the others were introduced by their relations, parents or friends. A few of them were deserted by husbands or lovers, one was raped and the others were forced. None of them had any specific skill though most of them had received some education. The younger lot who were new to the profession were not clear about the diseases of STD/HIV nor about the use of condoms. Though most of them (60 per cent) reported use of condoms but some said it was difficult to enforce.

Out of the 14 NGOs surveyed, 9 NGOs worked for the prevention of STDs/HIV among women and children and provided counselling; 8 NGOs were involved in educating women; 7 NGOs provided skill training; 6 NGOs were involved in providing financial help through loans, etc. ; 6 NGOs assisted in legal matters and none of the NGOs was found to be actively involved with perpetuation of child prostitution.

The brothel survey revealed that all brothels had preference for young women as they fetched higher price. Out of six, two brothels did not have any problem in keeping young girls while two bribed the police and two had problem with rowdies. None of the brothel-owners had been arrrested for illegal custody of minor girls. All the brothelowners were aware of STDs/HIV problem, yet they were not much concerned about the brothel inmates' health. Four of them claimed to send the women to private doctors regularly and also claimed to provide condoms to women. All claimed to provide financial help when the need required. All were of the view that the women had no escape from prostitution.

The government organisations surveyed revealed that they had one to 40 women in their care, all above 20 years of age. These organisations also provide counselling to the women after they had been arrested and charged.

The facts that emerged from the survey of 14 police stations was that the police was least interested in the age of women prostitutes or in verifying it. The girls under eighteen were generally sent back to their parents and rest to government remand homes. Nevertheless, facts charged by both the groups are same. The report states from the source of Home Ministry that out of total number of cases of rape one-third are committed against minors. The children, especially girls are at risk of sexual abuse by relatives, strangers, employers, head of the household and his sons, etc.

The report states that the number of child prostitutes is estimated to be 4,00,000 to 5,00,000 in India where the age of girl children ranges from 13-18 years. The lack of health-care services coupled with increasing demand for children in sex trade has put the children at higher risk for HIV and STD. According to the report the entry of girls under eighteen years of age is growing in Tamil Nadu. A large number of girls enter this trade voluntarily or through friends/parents to support their families.

Among the long list of recommendations given in the report some are the: involvement of village panchayats in education of community; consistent and continuous publicity on media regarding punishments to offenders restructuring of education systems to include training in vocational skills at secondary level; medical verification of age of children 'rescued' or 'committed' under prostitution laws; amendment of section 375 of the IPC, etc; children's rights to confidentiality with regard to their HIV status and separation of girls under eighteen from older women in institutions.

Goa: The 'Haven' of Sex Tourism

The study in Goa was inevitable as it has long been considered to be a "haven" for sex tourists and paedophiles. The study was carried out on the coastal belt (northern region) of Calangute, Candolim and Baiga. The research team followed observation and interview technique beside collecting secondary data.

The research team observed that children (both boys and girls) of the age group of 8-12 years resort to giving massages' to foreign tourists on the beaches or at their residence or hotels and gradually get lured into sexual encounters. It is reported that if the abused child is not rehabilited within six months then the child undergoes the vicious circle of guilt and abuse.

The exploiter may directly contact the child and after winning his/her trust finally carry out his ulterior motive. Then, contact with the child is also made indirectly, through parents. At times, parents takes the initiative and at other times the family is carried away by sham selflessness and benevolence shown by the exploiter and lets their child go with that person. If the child complains of the abuses faced by him the parents are not in position to punish the culprit because of faulty legal procedures and insensitive attitude. Procurers play their own role and are well versed with local dialects.

The place of abuse could be a rented room or residence. In any case, after the abuser's motive is achieved he shifts to some other place. The report says that the entire socio-legal system covers up the crime due to lure of the lucre in tourism and police turns a blind eye on such issues.

For south Goa, investigations were carried out on the beaches of Majorda, Colva and Benaulim. Interviews were carried out with hoteliers, shack owners, local people, school teachers and headmasters and stray children on beaches.

The investigation found that due to congestion on northern beaches, tourists are turning to southern Goa. Their modus operandi is well planned and systematic. Usually, an adolescent youth is taken into confidence with nice friendly talks and swims and thereafter asked to put sun tan lotion and then gradually and systematically approached to have sex.

The migrant labourers force their own children to earn some extra money under constraints of poverty and thereby disturbing their own children psychologically. When the children were interviewed they showed less interest in revealing everything to the investigator. Sixty per cent of them were not even aware that they are doing something wrong and the rest were at a loss for words.

The victims of paedophilia are well known to local people and shack owners but nobody has the courage to complain to the police. Local people told the investigators that there were night parties at weekends where the college going youth took part with foreigners and indulged in group sex during the tourist season. A case was reported where a fourteen-year-old girl was made a victim at such parties and was later blackmailed and forced to entertain four of the other tourists and in attending such more parties. Seventy per cent of the tourists carry cameras and photograph children without their clothes or while massaging. Foreigners seem more interested in boys than girls, therefore young boys are more vulnerable and in demand.

The red-light area of Baina houses some 2800 girls. Fifty per cent of these are "floating girls" who come on contract and the rest live with gharwalis or have rooms of their own. They fall in the age group of 12-16 years, and come from mainly Karnataka, Andhra Pradesh and Maharashtra. It is difficult to estimate the age of child prostitutes in Baina as the girls are made to lie about their age. The girls are brought from poor families of Karnataka, Andhra Pradesh, etc. Girl children of prostitutes are also inducted into the trade.

The investigator also found that most of the young girls from Karnataka belong to Devadasis and were brought to Goa on contract basis. Most of the girls are usually illiterate though some of them can write their native language. At least 90 per cent of them have serious health problems.

In the red-light area of Baina a few NGOs are working towards betterment of condition of prostitutes and their children by providing them education, vocational skills, creche facility, etc. The investigators reached the conclusion that to combat paedophilia, all foresgners needs to register themselves and the police and public should be more vigilant to catch any suspicious adult with a child. Not only by making laws more strict but also by their implementation, speedy justice is required to prevent trafficking and child prostitution. The report also recommended that schools should admit all children whether child prostitutes or children of prostitutes; monitoring cells needs to be put up in urban and rural areas to check inflow and outflow of children; gender sensitization is required. "Indira Awas Yojna" and ICDS government schemes should be extended to all red-light areas.

The Sex Workers in Rajasthan

When the investigator reviewed the earlier literature on child prostitution two main theories emerged. Consequently, the present study was conducted with specific objectives under the sponsorship of the National Commission for Women. The report proceeds with the definition of various terms leading to difference between the girl child prostitute and its adult counterpart.

Data was collected from 100 girl prostitutes belonging to Alwar, Bharatpur, Dholpur, Jaipur and Ajmer. Besides 50 various people were interviewed comprising police personnel, administrators, planners, social workers, academicians, etc. The research team visited prostitution-prone areas and recorded data through non-participant observation. The investigator admits that the report was compiled using primary and secondary data.

According to the report, Rajasthan has shown less social and economic development coupled with low literacy rate, lower status of girls and child marriage making the Rajasthani environment more conducive for social evils like prostitution to exist. Beside Rajasthan is known to host many castes practising prostitution traditionally since ancient and medieval times.

It is reported that there are 8,000 - 10,000 prostitutes in Rajasthan out of which 50-60 per cent are girl child prostitutes. The young prostitutes operate in both urban and rural areas of 15 districts of Rajasthan namely, Alwar, Ajmer, Baran, Bharatpur, Bundi, Bhilwara, Dholpur, Dousa, Dungapur, Jaipur, Jodhpur, Sawai Madhopur, Sirohi, Tonk and Udaipur.

The report describes the demographic features of these areas as higher population density, lower literacy rate which is even low for females and low economic conditions. The characteristic features of places of prostitution is reported to be the areas linked with national and State highways in the vicinity of "dhabas"(calling for larger floating population) and places where migrant males live alone and near places of large activity as business, commercial centres, etc.

Prostitution is practised in many forms in Rajasthan such as through brothels, by accompaning truck drivers, through hotels or by adopting traditional norms, characteristic of their respective caste/family. Different types of prostitutes flourishing in Rajasthan are common prostitutes, singing and dancing girls, concubines, call girls and hitch-hiking prostitutes.

The reasons for induction of girls into the trade has been reported to be social, cultural, economic, psychological, legal and administrative causes. The girls belonged to 10-18 years of age. They were mostly illiterate (95 per cent), lacked functional skills, belonged to economically deprived families and castes such as Bedias, Kanjars, Rajnats, Dholi, Dehredar and Grasi who practise prostitution as tradition.

These girls usually practise the trade for average 6-8 hours daily for 25-28 days per month. They may earn up to Rs. 150-200 per day after giving away commissions, etc. The clients they entertain are truck drivers, daily wagers, students and wealthy and powerful people. The castes which practise this trade as tradition usually train the girls from a tender age, much before their puberty. The impact of prostitution on these girls is felt in their health and emotional set-up. They suffer from low self-esteem and consider themselves different from other women.

There have been little efforts from government and no efforts from NGOs to rehabilitate these women and girls. The policies aimed at prostitutes should be of two types—rehabilitative and preventive. The report suggests that rehabilitative policies should aim at improving their quality of life by dissociating them from prostitute life, extending education, vocational training, legal facilities, etc. at residential or non-residential institutes. Preventive policies should aim at stopping entry of young girls into prostitution. It is suggested that this can be carried out by effective implementation of usual urban and tribal development programmes, improving standard of living of truckers and proper implementation of laws. Side by side, society should be sensitized towards this problem by making Panchayats actively involved in the procedure of planning.

West Bengal

The report states that trafficking of children from Bengladesh and Nepal and within the country as well has risen enormously. As many as 12-43 girls/women are trafficked each single day. Fifty per cent of girls and women practising in West Bengal brothels are from Bangladesh. West Bengal, because of its situation has become the central transit place for sending and receiving girls. Investigations revealed that the rate of increase of child prostitutes has risen directly in proportion to tourism. Due to AIDS younger virgin girls are more in demand.

The research team selected 70 child prostitutes at random from Sonagachi, Bowbazar, Kiddirpore, inmates of Liluah Government Home and Sanlaap Shelter. All the 70 prostitutes were interviewed of which 90 per cent of them were still working and 10 per cent were rescued by police. Eight per cent of the girls were Indians and belong to West Bengal, Madhya Pradesh and Uttar Pradesh; 10 per cent were Bangladeshi and rest 10per cent were from Nepal. They were of age group of 13-19 years.

According to the report regular pay-offs are given to the police by the brothelkeepers in the name of protection. Minor prostitutes are cross-checked in the very presence of their tormentors which holds them back from narrating their tragedies.

The Kalighaat area is as old as Calcutta. Initially women were kept for cooking and cleaning in small rooms for men who came for work alone in this city and hired these accommodation. Gradually, the system has changed and now 800 prostitutes live in area among whom 140 are "flying prostitutes". Girls from all over West Bengal, Nepal and Bangladesh are brought here. Prostitution is very open in this area. Prostitutes themselves are aware and do not shelter anti-social elements. In fact, they have helped police and NGOs in rescue of minor children from clutches of traffickers many times.

Bowbazar also has a history of 300 years. In this area about 3,000 prostitutes stay out of whom about 800 are "flying prostitutes". Girls from Nadia, Murshidabad, South 24-Parganas, Nepal and Bangladesh are brought here along with girls from Madhya Pradesh and Uttar Pradesh. Here, many child prostitutes could be found who work under ex-prostitutes that have turned into their keepers and who hold back all their income as well.

Sonagachi was established at the beginning of this century. Here, about 7000 prostitutes are present, 15 per cent of whom are "flying prostitutes". Girls are brought from Murshidabad, Nadia, 24-Parganas, UP, Bangladesh and Nepal. Child prostitutes are hidden in this area. It is estimated that they number about 13-15 thousand.

In all red-light areas women and girls mostly work as "adhyias" and "chukries", and are not in position to force their clients to use condoms. Consequently, they suffer from severe health problems such as tuberculosis, STDs, malnutrition, etc. The report states that child prostitutes who had worked for four years have had at least 4-6 abortions.

The report describes the pitiful conditions of child prostitutes who suffer from deep depression, rape, trauma, etc. Most of these children have been forced to have oral, anal and vaginal sex. It is very difficult for them to forget their past. When efforts are made to rehabilitate these children it is very difficult for them to fit into any healthy situation. They are refused the shelter of their respective homes and social stigma detaches them from any relationship. While working, these girls have to entertain 2-12 clients each night, thereby putting these children in terrible physical and mental conditions. Educational status of these girls is very poor rather nil and they are least aware of the STD, HIV/AIDS, abortions, stenilization, or family planning methods, etc. Gradually, the young girls becomes alcoholics.

Traffickers are both men and women. They have many helpers on the trafficking routes who assist them in crossing the border. Trafficking is more in specific period throughout the year during drought or during festival months or preharvest times. During this period traffickers use various ploys to lure girls and their parents.

The payments made per person is as follows:

Per Person		
Rs. 200/	Rs. 2000/-	To the Family
Rs.1000/	Rs. 2000/-	To the Procurer
Rs. 50/	Rs. 200/-	To the Police/BSF
Rs.1000/	Rs. 3000/-	To the Trafficker.

Traffickers generally drug the girls while transporting them from one place to other. Generally, poverty is known to be one of the major factors for induction of girls in this trade. Traffickers follow well-defined routes to cross borders. There are number of laws-both domestic and international to stop trafficking but all the laws concerning trafficking and prostitution have been misused or abused.

The report suggests many ways to tackle the problem of child prostitution and trafficking such as the involvement of panchayats, teachers, local doctors, etc., banning of child marriages, registration of all adult marriages; shelter homes with counselling and motivated programmes, orientation of police and judiciary and networking of national and regional NGOs. Further, the report suggests various activities in the red-light area for children of prostitutes belonging to various age groups. According to the report 2.3 million women are in prostitution of which a quarter are minors; 2000 prostitutes are Bangladeshi women four years back; 5000 girls are trafficked from Nepal every year.

The report sketches the description of Liluah home which provides shelter to children, victims of trafficking, prostitution, kidnapping, missing from home, etc. It is run by government in a pathetic state and is in dire need of bold and dynamic administration. Recently, because of involvement of Sanlaap, an NGO working in similar field, the situation has comparably improved.

On the lines of Liluah Home, Sanlaap had opened Sneha, which provides love, care and understanding to these children beside basic amenities. They have been enabled to repatriate six Nepali girls with help of Nepal NGO and more than 10 girls in Indian villages.

Andhra Pradesh

The study of Andhra Pradesh (AP) was carried out by 'AWARE' who are already doing their share of work in AP. The study was carried out in 11 out of 23 districts of AP and at 28 locations, three national highways, prisons and selected houses in Hyderabad. 170 prostitutes were interviewed belonging to different categories. The prostitutes are traditionally known as "Kalavanthulu" or "Bogam Vallu". They predominate in districts of east and west Godavari, Krishna and spread over is Srikakulam, Vijayanagram, Vishakhapatnam, Prakasam and Nellore. In the Telegana region they are called Devadasis, Matangees or Jogins. In Rayalaseema they are known as "Vesyalu" and "Basavi".

The report states that about 5,00,000 families in AP have prostitution as main occupation of which only 21 per cent want to leave the profession. The study indicated that 20 per cent enter this profession at very young age (5-11 years) and 47 per cent as minors (12-17 years). The research team found that victims of child prostitution mainly belong to Scheduled Caste and Backward communities (75 per cent). Most of them are illiterate (77 per cent). Culture is responsible for 18 per cent of child prostitutes whereas kidnapping, deception, adoption or selling contribute 60 per cent of child prostitutes. However, 15 per cent chose this line because of easy life and inclination. Though 70 per cent of prostitutes have children, only 38 per cent are unwed mothers.

The study revealed that 43 per cent of prostitutes earn less than Rs. 2000 per month of which half goes to brothelkeepers, police, pimps and goondas. Thrity per cent of prostitutes who have incomes less than Rs. 1000 live in great misery. Rest are call girls or urban prostitutes and earn between Rs. 2000-5000.

Roadside prostitution is rampant along the highways-Hyderabad-Mumbai-Vijayawada, Chennai and Hyderabad-Vijayawada. Small dhabas are located along the road on lonely stretches of road where girls (13-17 years old) from nearby villages make their appearance after dusk. They are unaware and uncaring of HIV/AIDS and most of them are infected with various STDs and tuberculosis. Only 23 per cent used condoms and 20 per cent said occasionally and hence most of them suffer from health problems. Dommara and Yerukalas dominate Telegana, Warangal, Nizamabad, Kainnagar, Medak and Nalgonda; Basavis in Kurnool and Ananthpur, and Jogins in Nizamabad, Adilabad, Karimnagar and Medak—all automatically qualifies for child prostitution as girls are inducted into the profession even before puberty. Call girls, street girls and prostitutes in brothel are generally confined to urban areas.

Many respondents (23 per cent) have migrated from their native place to the place of work because of natural calamity, in search of livelihood or ill-treatment by parent/family members while 60 per cent reported that they were deceived, kidnapped or sold.

It was revealed that 41 per cent women were married, 55 per cent were unmarried and 4 per cent were widows. Out of unmarried lot 38 per cent had children, i.e., they were unwed mothers. These women joined this line so as to support the family, education of children, insistence of husband, ill-treatment in the family, broken homes, marital maladjustments, dedication to God and caste profession and inclination towards easy life. The study shows that only 94/170 women were interested in vocational training while 23 women wanted to be self-employed. 110 women were such who were disgusted with the profession and wanted to leave it.

The report recommends some suggestions to combat the problem such as education, legal literacy, establishments of schools, development promotion, health education, legalization of prostitution by allocating area, providing medical support and identity cards, etc.

I am writing all this so that some day someone will read the situation and some of my young granddaughters-I would not be alive but can I help the **"Alive but dying within"** little buds of humans.

14

Awareness on Health Care

A young woman I know quite well, recently asked me rather hesitantly, if there was some easy way she could make out if her fiance had HIV. She didn't know how to discuss the issue but had heard enough about HIV/AIDS to be worried. I know the man in question—in fact have known him since he was a child actually and yet, I had to tell her that even I was not in a position to comment on his HIV status— or on anybody else's for that matter. And that is really the problem in this highly publicised issue of HIV/AIDS.

A little over 13 years ago, the HIV/AIDS virus was first identified in India and women in sex work were among the first people who were tested positive. The intervening years have seen this scenario change drastically. Today, "young respectably married" women are increasingly outnumbering almost any other population testing positive for HIV in India.

To take just take the case of my young friend who asked me a question very crucial to her life. In reply I asked if at all was it possible for her to ask her fiancé point-blank to test himself.

She said she could not imagine what her family and his would do even if she dared ask for any such thing. Queried whether she at least discuss her fears with her family? No, she did not know what to say and in any case, her parents thought the man and his family were a 'prize catch' and wanted her to get married to him. She was sure they would not do anything to rock the boat.

Today most young women in our society face the same dilemma. No matter how well educated, affluent, assertive and

---

For this Chapter I am indebted to Ms. Shyamala Nataraj, Chennai.

independent; sex, sexuality and sexual health both for women and for men continue to remain shrouded in an uneasy alliance of fear and shame and to an enormous cost.

For women this cost is proving to be doubly dear. A recent survey at a private hospital in Chennai which treats people with HIV related infections confirmed that the largest number of women showing up for treatment are married women with one sexual partner—their husband. Ironically one of the lowest figures belonged to women in prostitution—once again proving that women in prostitution are increasingly able to understand, accept and act towards protecting themselves.

Women in Prostitution

Almost 13 years ago women in prostitution were identified as the principal carriers of HIV in India. Ironically today they are among the lowest numbers testing positive for the rest of the world. The reasons have been several but the principal among them is their ability to accept their vulnerability to HIV infection and to adapt their behaviour accordingly. In the last several years successful interventions among women in prostitution has recognised this community bearing with strength in the face of enormous odds. Motivating the women to protect themselves as a direct expression of concerns for her well-being has been the single overriding cause for success. When women have been able to see themselves as important, capable, and participating in a process that helps others while helping themselves, they have responded magnificently. Different women have chosen different options—some have reduced the number of clients some others have looked for other avenues of income but the overwhelming majority have adopted safer sex practices and have persuaded clients to fall in line. These successes, however, have been won at the cost of intense support and entirely non-judgmental efforts by people concerned.

Shifting Vulnerabilities

It is now time to include the larger number of women outside prostitution who are increasingly more vulnerable to HIV infection simply because they have very little time to discuss their sexual life as also meagre support to deal with any problems in this area. These of course cannot be dealt independently from the context of their daily life.

In HIV prevention efforts give priority to lessening women's subordination so that they have more control over their own reproductive health. Policy-makers advocate effective STD treatment services usually targetted at commercial sex workers and male clients—and safer sex, including the use of condoms. But they are also faced with the inevitability of the woman having to ask the man to change his behaviour or use condoms and upon his refusal to do so, as well as the vulnerability of a monogamous married woman, she may not even know if she faces a risk because of her husband's behaviour.

The Mechanism of HIV

To begin with, a few fundamental facts about HIV need to be restated so as to understand the deeply traumatic impact it is having and shall continue to have on women and girl children in our country.

HIV is the human immune deficiency virus present principally in blood, semen and vaginal fluids. Entry of any of these infected fluids directly into the bloodstream of any individual leads to infection. Though HIV is also transmitted through infected blood, blood products or organs during transfusion or organ transplantation or even sharing or receiving injection drug equipment, over 90 per cent of all infections, particularly among women, remains due to unsafe sex.

But all this hype about HIV is meaningless unless there is a clear understanding about the fundamental reasons for the rapid spread of infections in this country. These are two fold. One is plainly related to the politics of gender and the other, while seemingly physiological in its appearance, is just as irrevocably driven by issues critical to women such as accessibility to resources, income sexuality and sexual freedom, health, education and social status, etc.

The Politics of AIDS

All women in India are silent and inert participant in an indirect conspiracy, may actually two, – misinformation on the one hand and silence on the other.

Let us start at the very beginning. In the early 1986, many of you probably woke up to find the newspapers announcing the arrival of AIDS in India. This was only partly true. What had really happened was that 14 people, all of them women, had tested positive for the HIV virus though none of them had AIDS.

While it was obvious to the meanest of intelligence that this skewed proportion was a direct relation of the sample tested – all 412 samples that had been tested belonged to women – it was conveniently interpreted that though AIDS was indeed here it was not likely to be a problem except for "immoral prostitutes" who probably deserved it anyway. Incidentally, all the women tested were at that time being held in remand homes around the State of Tamil Nadu under the Prevention of Immoral Traffic Act.

But worse was to follow. The women who had tested positive found that they were not released even after the expiry of their sentence period. The official view was that the women were a threat to society and that they would have to be locked up until such time a cure was found. A few months later, a batch of over 800 women arrived in Madras from Bombay on the assurance by the State Government that they would be sent back to their families. Instead, they were forcibly tested for HIV. Over 50 per cent of them tested positive for the virus.

The first conspiracy started then. It was one of misinformation where any discourse on AIDS was immediately closed with the single assumption that only women in prostitution were affected. It was therefore not very surprising that the news of the illegal detention of women did not raise any eyebrows. Such an attitude was expected and even condoned in the eyes of most people.

Fortunately some enlightened and concerned women brought the issues to the notice of the judiciary and the hapless women were released. Today no person can "officially" be held under detention because of the HIV status. I stress 'officially' because women continue to be held often on other flimsy charges if they are found positive for HIV. Most often these women are branded as prostitutes and the authorities feel they actually are doing society a good turn by holding them. Though of course nobody bothers to ask about the men who have infected these women in the first place, and continue to walk free.

The second conspiracy was one of silence. It began where the first left off. It is our simultaneous determination to not re-mystified sex, sexuality, sexual needs, behaviours and consequences that stem from the undeniable fact of our existence. Shrouded in an uneasy conspiracy of guilt, shame and fear, Indian women continue to remain silent and passively await the inescapable flood of infections that will certainly swamp them before long due.

How many of us know for instance that women are three to five times more likely to acquire HIV infection from a man than the other way around. This is because though the virus is present in both semen and vaginal fluids, the surface area of the vagina which is open to the infected semen is far greater than the surface area of the penis. Most women suffer from vaginal infections which may or may not be sexually transmitted. The symptoms for these may vary from white discharge, itching in the vagina, burning, pain during sex, or small sores or ulcers.

Many times we may even be unaware of these symptoms. Even if we are aware we are either ashamed to seek treatments or are ignorant about the facilities available. Such ignorance is immeasurably dangerous in the age of HIV. Usually such symptoms cause minute tears in the delicate, sensitive mucous membranes lining the walls of the vagina. These cause direct access to the virus into the bloodstream. HIV infection occurs only when the virus had direct entry into the bloodstream. For women, infections can also be introduced through unhygienic practices during child-birth or when contraceptive devices are inserted or removed.

An unhygienic IUD insertion can introduce infection. The tail of the IUD may also act as a conduit, taking infection from the vagina across the cervix to the upper reproductive tract. Sometimes women with signs of an infection attribute it to the contraceptive they are using and are even less likely to seek treatment.

The single most important reason why HIV is spreading so rapidly today is because there is already a very high level of untreated reproductive tract infections among women as well as men. Hardly anybody is aware of the meaning behind the symptoms, or the ways to deal with these effectively. In many places access to treatments may not be available. even where available there is a great deal of stigma attached to these issues. Worse, many doctors and nurses are condescending in their approach, unable to provide privacy or confidentiality and unwilling to educate the patient about safe sex including the use correct use of condoms.

Reproductive Health and HIV

Though there is a dispute about the origin of HIV, there is complete agreement about its relationship with reproductive tract infections, especially those that are sexually transmitted. The principal reason why HIV continues to spread almost at will is because of the high level of untreated sexually transmitted infections in the country. Much before the advent of HIV there have been documented levels of almost ten per cent of STDs incidence among sexually active people in India.

There is direct correlation between the presence of untreated STDs and the risk of HIV infection. Infection occurs largely when the virus directly enters the bloodstream of an individual. Untreated STDs are therefore open gateways for the virus as there is often presence of cuts, suppurations, ulcers and discharges in the genital area.

Women's vulnerability to STDs—and other reproductive tract infections (RTIs) not transmitted sexually—is increased by a whole array of physiological and social factors. Transmission rates of many STDs—including HIV are higher from men to women than vice versa. Many infections can occur without symptoms in women, and diagnosis is more difficult than for men. Fear of the social stigma that comes with admitting to this sort of health problem, combined with a lack of acceptable services for women, means treatment is less likely. As a result, they risk developing an infection of the upper reproductive tract (the womb and fallopian tubes) known as pelvic inflammatory disease (PID). This can lead to infertility, which can ruin lives or ectopic pregnancy—growth of the foetus in the fallopian tubes—which can be fatal if left untreated.

Some months ago I met a woman who had travelled from small town in Maharashtra to Bombay for treatment. She was 32 and already had three children when she noticed a "thick white discharge". Initially she ignored it, but when it continued she went to a 'private dispensary' where the doctor prescribed medication without conducting an examination. The problem persisted, so two months later she went to a government general hospital. Another course of medication was prescribed, which again did not help. Now, six months down the line, she had been referred to a health centre, where she had been told to come back the following week and get herself admitted for tests. "We may have to remove your 'birth bag' (uterus), so get somebody to arrange for three bottles of blood," she had been warned.

The World Health Organisation guidelines for the management of patients with STDs do not include hysterectomy—surgical removal of the uterus as an appropriate treatment. But I learnt that women routinely have a hysterectomy. "Most women come to us with advanced conditions... often the untreated infection has caused an acute case of pelvic inflammatory disease and in some cases we advise the removal of the uterus", said a doctor. "Unfortunately, many infections have no specific symptom other than vaginal discharge or irritation. Most women ignore them until (with some infection) it gets to a point where there is chronic abdominal or back pain and then they seek treatment."

A nationwide survey of existing STD facilities in June, 1990 by UNICEF revealed that there were virtually no facilities specially geared for women. This discouraged them from seeking treatment. Even in a city like Madras, there is only one trained STD woman doctor in the entire network of government hospitals. Undiagnosed and untreated infection of the cervix is one major cause for the increasing prevalence of cervical cancer which is one of the major killers of Indian women today.

This, however, is only one part of the problem. The other pertains to a woman's ability to prevent sexually transmitted infections and to demand sexual accountability and responsibility from her male partner. These questions are age-old and fundamental to an individual's existence. Yet they remain unasked or even when asked, unanswered.

Multiple jeopardy

What are the ways in which a woman can be affected. First, as a partner of an infected person with neither information nor resources nor power to protect herself. Second, as a single wage earner in the family as her husband progressively falls sick and loses ability to work. Third, as a source of further exploitation in the context of her lack of skills. Fourth as the principal care giver for her husband. Fifth as a single parent in the event of her husband's death.

And what if she herself is infected? All these scenarios have to be taken into account. Added to which she is most likely to be blamed as the cause of the problem in the first place. 'My son was perfectly well till he married you' is the commonest refrain.

Children and HIV

In a world encroached AIDS, there are children who are infected with HIV and as also those who are affected by the epidemic's intrusion into their families or communities. But the epidemic casts its biggest shadow by far on the hundreds of millions of children who live in risk of HIV infection because their fundamental rights, including the right to medical care and HIV information and education are ignored, or because their personal circumstances make them especially ignorant and vulnerable.

There is still no cure or effective vaccine for HIV, the virus that causes AIDS. In 1996 alone, 400,000 children under the age of 15 became infected with HIV, bringing the total number of children in this age group known to be living with the virus to 830,000 at the end of 1996. By the end of 1997, a million children under the age of 15 are expected to be living with HIV, with over 90 per cent of them in developing countries.

Because HIV infection often progresses quickly to AIDS in children, most of the close to 3 million children under 15 who have been infected since the start of the epidemic have developed AIDS, and a majority of them have died.

The vulnerability of girls to HIV infection is exacerbated by denial or neglect—including gender discrimination—-resulting in particular in low access to socio-economic opportunities. Commercial sexual exploitation and domestic sexual abuse of children are the contribution risk factors for HIV infection among children.

The figures reported to the 1996 World Congress against Commercial Sexual Exploitation of Children indicated that worldwide, more that 1 million children enter the sex trade every year. There are between 400,000 and 500,000 child prostitutes in India, according to a survey by India Today magazine. Research suggests that such exploitation is growing, and the age of children involved is falling.

Most children in the sex industry are girls aged between 13 and 18. Many such children spend most of their lives on the street, often because they are escaping violence or sexual abuse at home. Other children live in brothels having been drawn into prostitution by procurers.

Countless number of children worldwide are at risk of sexual abuse by relatives and other members of the child's community or strangers. The physical and mental abuse of children may increase the likelihood of their engaging in risk-taking sexual behaviour and thus increase their vulnerability to HIV. The HIV/AIDS epidemic has made child sexual abuse and abuse of children within prostitution more dangerous than ever before. Studies everywhere indicate that rate of HIV infection among child sex workers and street children are often very high.

The wrong belief that children are less likely to be infected has raised the demand for younger sex workers in recent years. The vulnerability of children to sexual exploitation, either through sex work or abuse, may well result in their becoming infected with other sexually transmitted diseases such as gonorrhea, syphilis and chancroid. By damaging the surfaces of the reproductive tract, physical trauma and sexually transmitted disease each of which increase the child's susceptibility to HIV as well as the HIV/STD risk to their clients. The problem is compounded by the lack of health-care services meeting the sexual and reproductive health needs of children.

Critical Imbalances

AIDS control efforts in India seem to suffer from critical imbalances. The most significant one is the inability or the unwillingness of most planners and implementing agencies to relate the issues of HIV prevention and control with reproductive health, particularly in the case of women.

As most activists rightly point out I am appalled at the continued focus on family planning alone. Are our women only brood mares? Do they have no other independent identity? Many woman have children later in life or may not have at all. Still others may be married and be deserted by their husbands or else widowed. I know for a fact that in many rural areas, unmarried adolescent girls are often victims of sexual abuse, either by their own family members or close friends and relatives. Are these women too not entitled to receive education and health care ? How best can we link the resources essential for reproductive health for all women with HIV control efforts?

What are the politics of allocations of the massively publicised National AIDS Control Programme. The spiralling rate of HIV infections suggests that these are largely dictated by the need for high profile activities that can generate the maximum amount of publicity for participants. Everytime there is a change of leadership either at the National/State level, there is another round of 'workshops' and 'seminars'. These are often held in five-star venues at enormous cost and inevitably include the same people who claim, to have been doing 'intensive' work for a long time.

The other equally unnecessary expense seems to be in the generation of publicity about AIDS. These messages appear too simplistic, often judgmental, and usually not applicable in the daily lives of people. I have seen hundreds of school children, 'March against AIDS'. What kind of example are we teaching them? First of all they are going to live in perpetual fear of people with AIDS, some of who might be themselves in a few years to come. Second, we are encouraging mouthing of platitudes without giving children any opportunity to understand the complex way in which the issue of HIV is inextricably bound with the issue of their own existence as human beings. I have seen balloons being let off with 'anti AIDS messages'. We are a nation supremely capable of reducing critical and complex issues into simple pictures of black and white. This is dangerous and is increasingly reflected in our inability to deal realistically with the problem.

Large amounts of money are now being spent on what I am told are 'targetted interventions.' The targets appear to be largely long distance workers, women in prostitution, and drug users. From all that I read and hear around the world, it appears that the virus has moved on. These populations were primarily at risk some years ago. Today vast numbers of ordinary men and women are even more at risk and little is being done to address this issue firmly and tactfully.

Finally the influence of international lending institutions that are insidiously affecting our social sector spending appears to be catching up with a vengeance in the area of HIV also. I have been routinely besieged by large number of people begging for help. They have included NGOs who have asked me to persuade authorities to release drugs, condoms, and other essential resources, women recounting tales of violence by family and society because they have tested positive, people begging for admission into hospitals for which they no longer have money to pay, children seeking seats in residential schools because their parents are either dead or dying. In each of these cases the reacting is discouragingly meagre and increasingly calls upon people to look after it themselves—an unrealistic and heartless response. This has led me to question if we are really serious about dealing with these as we claim to be.

Many Questions, Some Answers

Many of these questions continue to be asked. There are few answers but some strikingly simple are significant in their impact. First, no effective work can be done unless the rights guaranteed to every Indian under our Constitution are upheld. It seems more clear than even beore, that protection of human rights is a good way to ensure effective development. Where these rights are abused, it will be impossible to bring lasting and constructive change and will encourage spread of HIV/AIDS.

Secondly, most people, however uneducated, do understand the issues involved if they are given a chance to. This implies a climbdown from large scale, grandiose information campaign to grass roots activism, one to one, long to term work that includes not only the provision of access to concrete resources that can help people to use the information effectively. Thirdly, delinking of normative values around sexuality and sexual behaviours should come about.

Fourthly, working with women and men right from adolescence towards understanding their sexuality and sexual needs and responsibilities is required. And finally, acknowledging that HIV/AIDS is here to stay, at least for the foreseeable future, and adapting our responses towards accommodating and coping with the epidemic. We need to assimilate the people already touched by it as well as create means to also assimilate the countless others who will be in the years to come despite our best efforts.

15

Conclusions and Recommendations

The little girl in a chocked voice calls out and says "Ma I have not done anything, please let them not punish me". Time and again the victim is looked upon like a criminal. It is critical that laws should not be used against the victim but against the exploiters. On the one hand child traffickers force the children to offer their bodies and, on the other, the police lock them up in exploitative institutions in the name of rehabilitation. These homes are not a positive affirmation of the child's growth rather, the way the child is often treated here is as if it did something wrong is only a reaffirmation of the wrong-doing. The police only attack the symptom of the problem and not the causes.

Prostitution is one of the oldest, discernible and most condemned profession in the society. Further, rehabilitation of the sexually exploited individual is the most formidable but essential task ahead of us. The package of rehabilitation should be remunerative enough to attract and retain them on alternate vocations on giving up their profession and lead a normal life.

It is reported that a majority of women and children entering into this profession belong to the disadvantaged groups, such as the Scheduled Castes, the Scheduled Tribes (about 36.7 per cent), and the Backward Classes (24.24 per cent) while the remaining belong to the other category (39.9 per cent). Individuals in the profession can be categorized into two broad groups, i.e., those who joined this profession "willingly" and those "unwillingly". The former category could again be divided into two subcategories. i.e., those who are "hard core" and those who do not have any other means of livelihood. It is felt that "want of money" is the common factor which binds the two subcategories together.

While initiating the process of rehabilitation of women and children engaged in the profession we need to tackle them differently to suit each situation.

The women of "unwilling" category are most vulnerable. They are to be rescued from the clutches of "syndicates". Besides agents, they are forced into the profession by their relatives, friends and even husbands. Once rescued, proper protection should be provided to them to ensure security. This section of women and children may not need much persuasion to give up the profession once other means of livelihood are offered. The women belonging to "willing" category would need more persuasion and counselling especially the "hard core" types, because they are in the profession willingly and for easy money. Here, we may have to offer attractive means of livelihood for them to be economically independent.

The definition of 'child' has many versions in our Indian Penal Code (see Annexure—III). It is suggested that the definition of child in all laws should be redefined in India to include all persons below the age of 18 years. There is no provision in the law to implicate any adult, accused of causing sexual abuse on a small child such as paedophiles do. As has been cited in many cases in Goa, police is simply unable to hold any person in custody who is seen with a child under suspicious circumstances only because of absence of law. Hence, there is need for special laws which should specifically deal with all forms of sexual abuse other than penile penetration besides giving due effect to the Convention on the Rights of Children. Laws related to sexual offences against children should be made most stringent with penalties most severe imposed such as confiscation of property, castration, punishment to rapist in public.

The child who is victim of sexual abuse or exploitation is under great stress and trauma. To add to the child's problem, he/she is repeatedly exposed to the exploiter for sake of identification. It is grossly unfair for the child because just the sight of the exploiter is enough to trigger the mind back to the trauma she had passed through. The sight of the exploiter is sufficient for the child to destabilize her mind. Therefore, we strongly recommend that the information from the victim should be elicited in a closed room in the presence of a child psychologist, councillors, social workers and above all the camera. All the proceedings should be recorded. At the same time speedy justice should be provided to the victims. It is often seen that as the cases lie pending in the court the children and women are kept in remand homes or short stay shelters where these people are unable to mould their life into any channel because of the uncertainty of the future. At times they go out on bail and are again caught in the vicious circle. The opportunity to rehabilitate them or prepare them to join the mainstream is lost, especially children who had been inducted into the trade recently.

Many a time it is observed that police personnels refuse to register the First Information Report (FIR) as the complaint of victim is not supported with medical report, etc. It is recommended that FIRs should be immediately registered without waiting for any formalities. Further, cases of rape or sexual assault of an individual should not be judged solely on the criteria of medical examination. Sexual exploitation of a child in the name of custom, tradition and culture should be declared a punishable crime.

Today we are witness to the new phenomenon of sexual exploitation against children in the form of paedophilia—where children as small as five years are involved. Sometimes, parents are not aware of the intentions of the exploiters who presents himself as a "kind friend" and at other times parents themselves push the child into this deep well for some monetary needs. Children are usually too small to understand the intentions of his/her "friend" but at the same time allow himself / herself to be exploited in lieu of "wonder gifts" he/she received from "the friend". We, as adults, have a responsibility to prevent this vulnerable group of children for exploitation. Employment of children in sectors like tourism and hotels should be totally prohibited as it exposes the child to paedophiles and antisocial elements.

It is often seen that when girls are married at an early age, if they are deserted by their spouse or if they become widowed or if get separated from their husband, these young girls, most probably teenage mothers of small children are unable to stand on their own feet and support themselves and their children. Such women come under high risk group as they are easy targets for traffickers. This is the group of women which opts for the most loathsome profession voluntarily out of sheer desperation. At the young age these girls are uneducated and untrained for skills. As a result, to earn their livelihood, they may have little choice and may become either domestic servants, daily-wage labourers, etc. or prostitutes. If we are able to prevent entry of this group into the profession it will reduce the number of women in prostitution quite significantly. One of the preventive measures could be compulsory registration of all marriages like birth and death, among all religions alike. This step could prevent child marriages as well as discourage fake marriages. The second solution is education and mass awareness.

Education should be made compulsory and free for both boys and girls as literacy spreads general awareness, strength, economic empowerment as well as sense of judgment to differentiate between the right and the wrong. As no schools admit children of prostitutes it is strongly recommended that child prostitutes and children of prostitutes should be admitted in schools on the lines of Navodaya Vidyalayas. Adult education programmes should also include destitute women. This particular section of women and children need to be approached with lot of sincerity, compassion, kindness and lots and lots of patience. First, their mindset should be changed, then there is need to break their routine as their body is temporarily conditioned to have sex for above than 8-10 hours each day. This proves to be the greatest hurdle while rehabilitating them leaving beside the money factor. In one of the reports from Goa it was observed that if the sexually abused child is not rehabilitated within seven months then it is very difficult to gain success in such a case. The parents should be provided incentives to send their children to school. Then, value of education should be promoted among public through media, plays and various other educational programmes.

These children and women need dedicated efforts of health professionals such as gynecologists, psychologists and social workers. These health care professionals should be encouraged and held responsible to the concerned authorities to facilitate an early identification of the exploiters. Whenever, attending to the abused child they should try to take the child into confidence and extract the total information as a routine and at the same time should provide a healing touch to their bruised egos. The health care professionals should counsel the child and women about the various health problems faced by their counterparts in this profession such as STDs, HIVs/AIDS etc. and about their preventive methods as well. The abused children and women should be taken into confidence before testing for HIV, AIDS, etc.

Along with education, vocational training and health care counselling, self-defence skills and unarmed combat classes should also be held especially in girls schools.

The government could play an important role for upliftment of this section. The government should act as a catalyst and facilitator for the implementation of rehabilitation programmes and should monitor them periodically for their successful implementation. It should provide resources and infrastructure in the critical areas of development such as health services, education, vocational training and above all shelter homes. It should ensure by various means that the resources allocated for particular sector reaches the beneficiaries intact by proper implementation of its programmes and should carry out its policies and programmes, particularly for this sensitive group in coordination with proper assistance of National Commission for Women, State Commissions for Women and NGOs working in this area. At the same time government should give more teeth to NCW and other State Commissions and NGOs as well to keep close vigil on rehabilitation programmes and shelters so as to achieve success in rehabilitating the women and children at the earliest. Only government in coordination with NGOs, and grass roots bodies as Panchayats, etc. can ensure education to this vulnerable group by extending proper facilities and appropriate resources. Recently, the Department of Women and Child Development and Welfare Ministry had initiated many programmes for the girl child, but no programmes for children in prostitution had been chalked out separately.

A grievance cell should be created and needs to be monitored by NCW and Department of Women and Child Development where complaints regarding the commercial exploitation of children can be lodged and thereafter, such complaints could be handed over to media and disciplinary authorities for necessary actions.

Often there is a feeling that police are in "hand-in-glove" relationship with the traffickers, pimps and brothelkeepers. The government should take effective measures to break the above mentioned nexus between police and perpetrators of crime. The police are often callous and rude towards the women and children. They raid the brothels initially posing as customers, harass the inmates and when they receive their due "hafta" act as their protectors also. They are also accused of receiving sexual favours from them without payment. At times they are accused by these women of forcing them to carry on the trade for them, in police stations as well. There is need to sensitize police personnel regarding the laws and issues of prostitution and trafficking. They should especially be instructed while handling women and children. The filing and investigation of the report should be completed within 90 days. As the case loses its importance, the evidences are tampered and many changes occurs from the time of crime to initiation of investigations.

Though networking of traffickers is very well established yet it remains hidden from police. Various trafficking routes, supply, transit centre/countries should be identified by the police by working in close coordination with national and international agencies. At the same time there is need to establish strong networking among the police, NGOs, village panchayats and State administration in order to build an information data base in conjunction with interpol and CBI.

As one of the preventive measures, the police should keep a close eye on all those foreigners who stay for long periods without any apparent occupation; who visit the same place repeatedly as tourists; who display any abnormal behaviour or look suspicious.

For rescue, rehabilitation and prevention beside the government, police and state a major role would be played by the community and grass roots bodies such as village panchayats, teachers, anganwadi workers, etc. The active participation of community at large is a must to prevent recruitment of new girls into this system. As has been mentioned earlier the cultural and traditional prostitution in the name of religion are practised by and large with the sanction from community. The dedication of girls before or at puberty should be completely banned. Though the Act regarding Devadasi system for prohibition of girls was passed long time back but its implementation lies in the hands of community. Then, the tribals who had been practising prostitution as their only occupation should be discouraged. As mentioned earlier they practise this trade near roadside in dhabas, as " floating prostitutes" and of course in brothels. Thereby, in a way they spread wrong signals to the men seeking sex that all girls seen alone are available for their perverse desires. This practice needs to be stopped by providing these people alternate means of livelihood, education, etc. The community should be empowered through specific mechanisms such as representatives and responsible bodies. At the village level these bodies should include panchayats, women's group, NGOs, school teachers, community leaders and stockholders.

The first and foremost task of the community should be to eliminate gender discrimination. The oppression of girl child leads to her being illiterate, unskilled, unaware, with no confidence and forever dependant—financially, morally and physically. Secondly, the community needs to change men's psyche. When the man will change his attitude towards woman, he will no longer consider her as a mere sex object and at the same time if girl is able to stand on her own she will resist and could rebel against the degrading attitude of men. Therefore, the parents, youths and society at large should be sensitized on the issue of gender discrimination. Thirdly, representative bodies of communities like panchayats need to be actively involve in keeping an eye on all villagers especially children belonging to high risk group. They should immediately report the missing of any child or woman in their respective area to the concerned authorities. Likewise, teachers, social workers, and anganwadi workers should also keep vigil on children and should report to panchayats or concerned authorities about the missing child or even about the change in attitude of children. It has been seen and observed in many cases in Goa that once the child has been with paedophiles or in other words has been sexually abused he or she start behaving as an adult. Only vigilant teachers could differentiate in their behaviour and way of dressing up.

Fourthly, village panchayats should play an active role in reducing prostitution through religious sanctions. The panchayat should be held responsible for the Devadasi children and should refer them to appropriate authorities. These panchayats should also make sure that there are no benami transactions and the Devadasis are the rightful owners of the land allotted to them.

It has been reported repeatedly, that the traffickers usually belong to same or nearby village and are often familiar with the family of children. Sometimes ex-prostitutes come to their native places to recruit new girls. They lure the girls by display of jewellery, cosmetics and fling money by throwing feasts for the whole village. Here, panchayats need to look into the matter. Once the purpose of such visitors becomes obvious, the children should be protected from their clutches and such people should be ostracized by the panchayat and thereby by the community. Further, the trafficker should be imposed with heavy fine on compensatory grounds to the victim's family, so as to discourage such future activities.

There is a need to have a monitoring agency with the specific task of liaising with various agencies to look after the welfare of society, to prevent induction of new girls into the trade and to stop trafficking. The dedicated fit into this role best. NGOs are the best grass roots bodies who could play significant role in rescue, rehabilitation and prevention of young girls and boys. They have the privilege to reach out to remote villagers as well as to the administrative bodies alike. They could play an instrumental role in spreading awareness among the most vulnerable group regarding the modus operandi used by traffickers and pimps to recruit new young and innocent girls.

NGOs could collate all the laws relating to prostitution and document success stories of rehabilitation to the potential candidates while imparting counselling to them. They can also run schools, vocational training centres and can also help the women to collect together and form cooperatives or self-help groups so as to generate income and enable these women to be financially independent. The products prepared by these girls and women should be marketed with assistance from various industries and State Governments. NGOs could also arrange health camps for these women periodically and keep these women abreast of their latest health status— such camps will spread general health awareness beside enabling the women to guard themselves from various STDs, HIV,AIDS and other health problems.

NGOs with good track record and social commitment working in coordination with state administration should be persuaded and entrusted with job of rehabilitating young girls and women in prostitution.

The efforts of government, community and NGOs if assisted by media can reach far in short period. Media is a best and effective way to mobilize people at grass roots level with latest technology and if by portable mediums the remotest corner of earth is approachable then why not the remotest village which is the target group of traffickers and resource of new victims. Media should spread awareness against child prostitution and trafficking by constantly displaying visuals with simple but clear messages but at the same time they should be careful in not portraying children in compromising, illegal or pornographic situations. Media should campaign to demolish myths on sex with children. It can help in revealing trafficking operations for public through news, plays, skits, etc. as often as possible and should publicize the follow-up actions in similar manner. It should highlight that it is always not "easy money" in this trade but it cost one's social life, health status, and carries a curse for one's children all through the life.

Recently, the NCW had been experimenting with the senior and ex-prostitutes, who were motivated conscientiously about the necessity of rescue and rehabilitation of women in prostitution, more especially a girl child. These women were counselled and educated on the issue that minor girls instead of curing dreadful diseases are more vulnerable to such diseases. Then, it was explained to them that when young girls are allowed in the brothels they fetch more price than their senior counterparts. So, if entry of younger ones is restricted they could earn more. They had been encouraged more and more to report the matter to the social worker, volunteers or to the honest police personnel. NCW had some success in this experiment. After receiving information the brothels and other places where children are hidden could be rescued by raiding those places.

The girls once rescued should be given good psychotherapy, counselling and medical treatment to boost their bruised egos and to uplift their morals. Once they are on their way of normalization they should be admitted to usual schools without disclosing their identities. Their mental capability should be assessed and accordingly they should be coached for vocational skills so as to equip them for better jobs. Rescued girls should be integrated with other girls for bringing them into the mainstream of society.

At this juncture, it is very important to mention that employees in shelter homes, nari niketans or short stay homes and most of the people dealing with them are generally very rude to the inmates. They again and again treat this particular section with contempt and subject them to discrimination, social isolation and deprive them of normal life for no fault of their own. These people fail to understand that these young children and women are only victims of shocking sexual abuse and of circumstances and hence should be treated as human beings like others so as to bring them into the mainstream without stigma. They needs to be treated with compassion and understanding.

Not only employees of remand homes but also the police, the medical professionals, judiciary and lawyers need to be sensitized to the cause of victims and about the ways to handle them.

Further, for the rescued girls and women in remand homes who are undertrial, their cases should not be delayed in court rather speedy justice should be given to them, because often it has been seen that the brothelkeepers, pimps and traffickers find the way to reach them and bail them out continue the trade. Secondly, while in remand homes these girls and women are not put under any rehabilitative programmes and they are again drawn towards the profession.

When any person presents himself/ herself as parent / guardian of the abused child to seek her/his custody from the police or court the child should not be handed over to them without proper verification. Many NGOs have reported that brothelkeepers and traffickers present themselves as parents/guardians. When the child is asked to verify them, they do what they are told to as the very sight of them is enough for the child to think back the miserable time she/her had gone through. It is suggested that in case of parents at least, simple forensic tests could be performed like blood group tests, dermataglyphic tests, etc. so as to establish the relationship between the two. In case of guardian proper verification should be done.

It is also recommended that whenever the rehabilitative programmes are being formulated they should not be bound by time as it affects the efficiency of the programmes.

The rescued girls and the ones who want to give up the profession should be properly counselled and encouraged to part with their traumatic experiences and preach the vulnerable group and her family. They should go back to their native villages and to further remote areas and with the help of NGOs should identify the traffickers, who may be natives of the same villages and should warn the villagers against falling prey to them. They should also convince those girls who think this trade gives "easy money" without realising at what cost.

Trafficking has become an international nuisance. On one hand Nepal appears to be the most significant, identifiable source of child prostitute for Indian brothels and on the other hand Bangladesh seems to provide resource of children and women to the Middle East and some Asian countries. It is reported that approximately, 5000 - 7000 Nepali girls under the age of 18 years are trafficked into India annually. After crossing border they are deported to various Indian brothels across the country. In Bangladesh, agents lure the parents, guardians, women with the promise of big money through advertisements for domestic job across the border.

It is strongly recommended that the Indian Government should negotiate with SAARC countries particularly Nepal, Bangladesh and Sri Lanka to effectively prevent the migration or transport of children for sexual abuse in India. Each country should enact legislations whereby their citizens are punishable for the offences, related to sexual abuse and trafficking they have committed in another country.

There is need to identify the risk groups and their data be compiled, kept updated and information shared internationally on a regular basis. State and national level representatives of international organizations such as the World Tourism Organization, International Union of Food, and hotel management organizations should be urged to take necessary actions.

The NCW has recommended that a bureau on the lines of the Narcotics Bureau should be set-up at the borders to stop trans-border trafficking.

To curb trafficking and paedophilia, sex tourism should be curbed by close association of the government, municipal councils, village panchayats, educational and religious institutions. Child trafficking entails proper safeguards, including independent monitoring and follow-up. For children to be returned to their country of origin, they should not be treated as illegal immigrants by the receiving countries but dealt with humanely as special cases of humanitarian concern upon the children's return, the countries of origin should treat them with respect in accordance with international human rights principles.

The rescued women and children should be immediately put in the institutions or protective homes or appropriate shelters to give them a sense of participation. These institutions should be equipped enough to provide these women and children shelter, security, mental peace, care, clothing, food, education, vocational training, facility for counselling, recreation, etc. These institutions should assume responsibility for reporting the number of women and children admitted and in their care to the district administration, periodically so as to enlist their help in giving them proper protection from any outside element who could attempt to coerce or harass. Also, social workers and NGOs must be invariably entrusted with the task of rescue and rehabilitation. These institutions should have the benefit of monitoring by agencies such as NGOs, Women and Child Development Department, NCW and State Commissions and should motivate government to take up the issues at higher levels. These organizations should be able to extend benefits of policies and schemes to the women in an optimum manner.

ANNEXURE–I

Reports Sponsored by NCW, Govt. of India

1. Societal Violence on Women and Children in Prostitution 1995-96, NCW, 4, Deen Dayal Upadhyaya Marg, New Delhi- 110002.
2. Commercial Sex Workers of Andhra Pradesh, 1997, AWARE, Development Research Advisory Group, 5-9-24, 78, Lake Hill Road, Hyderabad-500463.
3. Child Prostitution in Karnataka, Some Observations by a Social Work Educator, 1997, Karnataka State Commission for Women.
4. Child Abuse and Prostitution in Tamil Nadu, 1997, Women AIDS Action Development Society, Tricky and South India AIDS Action Programme, Chennai.
5. A Study of Child Prostitution in West Bengal, 1997, Indrani Sinha and SANLAAP, 21B, Pratapaditya Road, Calcutta 700026.
6. Lost Childhood, The First Study of Child Prostitution in India, 1997, Roma Debabrata.
7. Girl Child Prostitution in Rajasthan Policies and Programmes, 1997, Mukherjee, K.K., Davika, T.K. and Mukherjee, M., Gram Niyojan Kendra, Ghaziabad, U.P.
8. The Velvet Blouse, by Dr. (Mrs.) Mohini Giri, Sexual Exploitation of Children, 1997, NCW, 4 Deen Dayal Upadhyaya Marg, New Delhi - 110002.
9. Girl Child Prostitution in India (Policies and Programmes), 1997, Gram Niyojan Kendra, Ghaziabad, U.P.
10. Girl Children in Prostitution, Cases from Kerala, 1997, Kerala Women's Commission, Loyala Extension Services, Loyola College of Social Sciences, Sreekayam, P.O. Thiruvananthapuram- 695017, Kerala.
11. Study Report on Sexual Abuse of Children in Goa, 1997, Desterro Eves Mahila Mandal, c/o Atao Residence, Near M.P.T. Hospital, Vasco-da-gama, Goa - 403802.

12. National Consultation on Sexual Exploitation of Children, 1997, 23-24 July, Panaji, Goa.
13. A Study of Women and Girls in Prostitution in Orissa : Their Needs, Problems and Perspectives, 1996, Jewan Rekha Parisha (JRP), N-1/78, I.R.C. Village, Nayapalli, Bhubaneswar-751015, Orissa.
14. Report on the State-level Workshop on Sensitisation for and Rehabilitation of Children Exploited for Commercial Sex, 1997, Council for Social Development and All India Women's Conference, Jaipur.
15. Midnight Angels by Dr. (Mrs.) V. Mohini Giri.

ANNEXURE–II

International Conventions and Legal Provisions

Articles 1 and 2 of the 1949 Convention for the Suppression of Traffic in Persons provide that States shall:-

> punish any person who, to gratify the passions of another : procures, entices or leads away, for purposes of prostitution, another person, even with the consent of that person, (and) any person who keeps or manages or knowingly finances or takes part in the financing of a brothel, knowingly lets or rents a building or other place or any part thereof for the purposes of the prostitution of others.

Article 17 of the 1949 Convention states that the States shall endeavour-

(a) to make regulations for the protection of immigrants and emigrants, in particular women and children at places of departure and arrival;

(b) to arrange for appropriate publicity warning the public of the dangers of trafficking;

(c) to take measures for the supervision of railway stations, airports, seaports and of other public places in order to prevent international traffic in persons for purposes of prostitution;

(d) to create mechanisms and procedures which would allow appropriate authorities to be informed of the arrival of persons who appear prima facie, to be traffickers or victims of traffic.

The 1949 Convention for the Suppression of the Traffic in

Persons and the Exploitation of the Prostitution of Others (The Convention) is a good beginning in an attempt to understand what trafficking in women is. The Convention defines trafficking in persons as procuring, enticing or leading away, for purposes of prostitution, another person, even with the consent of that person. The Convention was, of course, recognizing the fact that not just women are trafficked, although women do form 99 per cent of the victims of trafficking in persons. Other international instruments and human rights documents, though referring and/or applying to trafficking in women, do not define it. Article 6 of the Convention on the Elimination of All Forms of Discrimination Against Women, for instance, mandates all State parties to suppress all forms of traffic in women and exploitation of the prostitution of women without defining either concept. Similarly, Article 2(b) of the United Nations Declaration on the Elimination of Violence Against Women, without defining trafficking in women and forced prostitution, regards it as a form of violence against women, which should be eliminated. Para 18 of the Vienna Declaration and Program of Action of 1993 also refers to international trafficking as a form of sexual exploitation but offers no definition of international trafficking.

Further insight into the meaning of trafficking in women can be found in various national legislations. The Dutch Penal Code, for instance, provides that a person is guilty of traffic in persons when he :-

1. forces another person into prostitution by mean of:
   - (a) violence; or
   - (b) the threat of violence; or
   - (c) by abusing the authority or ascendancy derived from actual relationship; or
   - (d) by misleading another person or by deception; or when he
2. does anything under circumstances knowing or reasonably suspecting that the other person will thereby end up in prostitution.

In Thailand, under the Trafficking in Women and Girls Act, any person who brings women or girls into Thailand for the purposes of having sexual intercourse with other persons and any other person who is involved illegally in the trading of women or girls brought into the country for such purposes, commits an offence. In Uganda, trafficking, referred to as procurement is indicated as follows :

Any person who -

(a) procures or attempts to procure any girl or woman under the age of 21 years to have unlawful carnal connection, either in Uganda or elsewhere, with any person or persons; or
(b) procures or attempts to procure any woman or girl to become either in Uganda or elsewhere a common prostitute; or
(c) procures or attempts to procure any woman or girl to leave Uganda, with intent that she may become an inmate or frequent a brothel elsewhere; or
(d) procures or attempts to procure any woman or girl to leave her usual place of abode in Uganda, (such place not being a brothel), with intent that she may, for the purposes prostitution, become an inmate of, or frequent a brothel either in Uganda or elsewhere.

Commits an Offence

In India the existing provisions under the Immoral Traffic (Prevention) Act, 1956 (hereinafter called the Act) defines "child" as a person who has not completed the age of sixteen years. According to the Act, any person who keeps and manages and acts assists in the keeping and management of, a brothel shall be punishable on first conviction with rigorous imprisonment for a term of not less than one year and not more than three years and also with fine which may extend to two thousand rupees and in the event of second conviction it will be more.

Further the Act also provides punishment for persons who lives on the earnings of prostitution. The Act also provides punishment for those who procure induce and take and detain persons for the sake of prostitution. Furthermore the Act prohibits the carrying on of prostitution in the vicinity of public places.

The Act also contains discriminatory provisions like providing of more punishment to the women, while compared with men for the acts of seducing or soliciting for purposes of prostitution. Further the Act gives special powers to the Central Government for the constitution / establishment of special courts for the speedy trial of offences under this Act. The said court is also empowered to try the cases summarily. Furthermore the government can also appoint trafficking police officers to deal with such specific cases.

ANNEXURE–III

Legal Definition of the Child

Criminal Law Indian Penal Code, 1860: Nothing is an offence which is done by a child under seven years of age (*Section 82*). Nothing is an offence which is done by a child above seven years of age and under twelve, who has not attained sufficient maturity of understanding to judge the nature and consequences of his conduct on that occasion. (*Section 83*).

Juvenile Law: The Juvenile Justice Act, 1986: Juvenile means a boy who has not attained the age of sixteen years or a girl who has not attained the age of eighteen years.

Family Law Child Marriage Restraint Act, 1929: 'Child' means a person, who, if a male, has not completed twenty-one years of age and if a female, has not completed eighteen years of age.

Labour Laws Apprentices Act, 1961: A person shall not be qualified to be engaged as an apprentice ... unless he is not less than fourteen years of age.

Factories Act, 1948: No child who has not completed his fourteen years of age shall be required or allowed to work in any factory.

Mines (Amendment) Act, 1983: No person below eighteen years of age shall be allowed to work in any mine or a part thereof.

The Child Labour (Prohibition and Regulation) Act, 1986 : 'Child' means a person who has not completed his fourteenth year of age.

Appendix III

Legal Definition of the Child

[illegible] Indian Penal Code, [illegible] is done by [illegible] years of age [illegible] attained sufficient maturity of understanding to judge the nature and consequences of his conduct on that occasion. [illegible]

[illegible] Juvenile [illegible] 1986 [illegible] has not attained the age of eighteen years.

[illegible]

[illegible]

[illegible]

[illegible]

[illegible]

Annexure–IV

Sexual Offences

Section 375, Indian Penal Code: Rape—A man is said to commit "rape" who, except in the case hereinafter excepted, has sexual intercourse with a woman under circumstances falling under any of the six following descriptions :-

First — Against her will.

Secondly — Without her consent.

Thirdly — With her consent, when her consent has been obtained by putting her or any person in whom she is interested in fear of death or of hurt.

Fourthly —With her consent, when the man knows that he is not her husband, and that her consent is given because she believes that he is another man to whom she is or believes herself to be lawfully married.

Fifthly — With her consent when, at the time of giving such consent, by reason of unsoundness of mind or intoxication or the administration by him personally or through another of any stupefying or unwholesome substance, she is unable to understand the nature and consequences of that to which she gives consent.

Sixthly —With or without her consent, when she is under sixteen years of age.

Explanation: Penetration is sufficient to constitute the sexual intercourse necessary to the offence of rape.

Exception: Sexual intercourse by a man with his own wife, the wife not being under fifteen years of age, is not rape.

Section 376, Indian Penal Code Punishment for rape—(1) Whoever, except in the cases provided for by sub-section(2) commits rape shall be punished with imprisonment of either description for a term which shall not be less than seven years but which may be for life or for a term which may extend to ten years and shall also be liable to fine unless the woman raped is his own wife and is not under twelve years of age, in which case, he shall be punished with imprisonment of either description for a term which may extend to two years or with fine or with both:

Provided that the court may, for adequate and special reasons to be mentioned in the judgement, impose a sentence of imprisonment for a term of less than seven years.

(2) Whoever,

(a) being a police officer commits rape-

(i) within the limits of the police station to which he is appointed; or

(ii) in the premises of any station house whether or not situated in the police station to which he is appointed; or

(iii) on a woman in his custody or in the custody of a police officer subordinate to him; or

(b) being a public servant, takes advantage of his official position and commits rape on a woman in his custody as such public servant or in the custody of a public servant subordinate to him; or

(c) being on the management or on the staff of a jail, remand home or other place of custody established by or under any law for the time being in force or of a women's or children's institution takes advantage of his official position and commits rape on any inmate of such jail, remand home, place or institution; or

(d) being on the management or on the staff of a hospital, takes advantage of his official position and commits rape on a woman in that hospital; or

(e) commits rape on a woman knowing her to be pregnant; or

(f) commits rape on a woman when she is under twelve years of age; or

(g) commits gang rape,

shall be punished with rigorous imprisonment for a term which shall not be less than ten years but which may be for life and shall also be liable to fine:

Provided that the court may, for adequate and special reasons to be mentioned in the judgement, impose a sentence of imprisonment of either description for a term of less than ten years.

Explanation 1. Where a woman is raped by one or more in a group of persons acting in furtherance of their common intention, each of the persons shall be deemed to have committed gang rape within the meaning of this subsection.

Explanation 2. "Women's or children's institution" means an institution, whether called an orphanage or a home for neglected women or children or a widows' home or by any other name, which is established and maintained for the reception and care of women or children.

Explanation 3. "Hospital" means the precincts of the hospital and includes the precincts of any institution for the reception and treatment of persons during convalescence or of persons requiring medical attention or rehabilitation.

Section 376A, Indian Penal Code. Intercourse by a man with his wife during separation—Whoever has sexual intercourse with his own wife, who is living separately from him under a decree of separation or under any custom or usage without her consent shall be punished with imprisonment of either description for a term which may extend to two years and shall also be liable to fine.

Section 376B, Indian Penal Code. Intercourse by public servant with woman in his custody. Whoever, being a public servant, takes advantage of his official position and induces or seduces, any woman, who is in his custody as such public servant or in the custody of a public servant subordinate to him, to have sexual intercourse with him, such sexual intercourse not amounting to the offence of rape, shall be punished with imprisonment of either description for a term which may extend to five years and shall also be liable to fine.

Section 376C, Indian Penal Code. Intercourse by superintendent of jail, remand home, etc.— Whoever, being the superintendent or manager of a jail, remand home or other place of custody established by or under any law for the time being in force or of a women's or children's institution takes advantage of his official position and induces or seduces any female inmate of such jail, remand home, place or institution to have sexual intercourse with him, such sexual intercourse not amounting to the offence of rape, shall be punished with imprisonment of either description for a term which may extend to five years and shall also be liable to fine.

Explanation 1. "Superintendent" in relation to a jail, remand home or other place of custody or a women's or children's institution includes a person holding any other office in such jail, remand home, place or institution by virtue of which he can exercise any authority or control over its inmates.

Explanation 2. The expression "women's or children's institution" shall have the same meaning as in Explanation 2 to subsection (2) of section 376.

Section 376D Indian Penal Code: Intercourse by any member of the management or staff of a hospital with any woman in that hospital. Whoever, being on the management of a hospital or being on the staff of a hospital takes advantage of his position and has sexual intercourse with any woman in that hospital, such sexual intercourse not amounting to the offence of rape, shall be punished with imprisonment of either description for a term which may extend to five years and shall also be liable to fine.

Explanation. The expression "hospital" shall have the same meaning as in Explanation 3 to subsection (2) of section 376. Extracts from the Code of Criminal Procedure, 1973 (2 of 1974).

Section 46 : Arrest How Made

(1) In making an arrest the police officer or other person making the same shall actually touch or confine the body of the person to be arrested, unless there be a submission to the custody by word or action.

(2) If such person forcibly resists the endeavour to arrest him, or attempts to evade the arrest, such police officer or other person may use all means necessary to effect the arrest.

(3) Nothing in this section gives a right to cause the death of a

person who is not accused of an offence punishable with death or with imprisonment for life.

Section 54: Examination of arrested person by medical practitioner at the request of the arrested person. When a person who is arrested, whether on a charge or otherwise, alleges, at the time when he is produced before a Magistrate or at any time during the period of his detention in custody that the examination of his body will afford evidence which will disprove the commission by him of any offence or which will establish the commission by any other person of any offence against his body, the Magistrate shall, if requested by the arrested person so to do direct the examination of the body of such person by a registered medical practitioner unless the Magistrate considers that the request is made for the purpose of vexation or delay or for defeating the ends of justice.

Section 160: Police Officer's Power to Require Attendance of Witnesses

(1) Any police officer making an investigation under this Chapter may, by order in writing require the attendance before himself of any person being within the limits of his own or any adjoining station who, from the information given or otherwise, appears to be acquainted with the facts and circumstances of the case; and such person shall attend as so required:

Provided that no male person under the age of fifteen years or woman shall be required to attend at any place other than the place in which such male person or woman resides.

(2) The State Government may, by rules made in this behalf, provide for the payment by the police officer of the reasonable expenses of every person, attending under sub-section (1) at any place other than his residence.

Section 309: Power to Postpone or Adjourn Proceedings

(1) In every inquiry or trial the proceedings shall be held as expeditiously as possible, and in particular, when the examination of witnesses has once begun, the same shall be continued from day to day until all the witnesses in attendance have been

examined, unless the court finds the adjournment of the same beyond the following day to be necessary for reasons to be recorded.

(2) If the court, after taking cognizance of an offence, or commencement of trail, finds it necessary or advisable to postpone the commencement of, or adjourn, any inquiry or trial, it may, from time to time, for reasons to be recorded, postpone or adjourn the same on such terms as it thinks fit, for such time as it considers reasonable, and may by a warrant remand the accused if in custody:

Provided that no Magistrate shall remand an accused person to custody under this section for a term exceeding fifteen days at a time:

Provided further that when witnesses are in attendance, no adjournment or postponement shall be granted, without examining them, except for special reasons to be recorded in writing :

Provided also that no adjournment shall be granted for the purpose only of enabling the accused person to show cause against the sentence proposed to be imposed on him.

Explanation 1. If sufficient evidence has been obtained to raise a suspicion that the accused may have committed an offence, and it appears likely that further evidence may be obtained by a remand, this is a reasonable cause for a remand.

Explanation 2. The terms on which an adjournment or postponement may be granted include, in appropriate cases, the payment of costs by the prosecution or the accused.

Section 437: When Bail may be taken in case of Non-bailable Offence.

(1) When any person accused of, or suspected of the commission of any non-bailable offence is arrested or detained without warrant by an officer in charge of a police station or appears or is brought

before a court other than the High Court or Court of Session, he may be released on bail, but -

(i) such person shall not be so released if there appear reasonable grounds for believing that he has been guilty of an offence punishable with death or imprisonment for life;

(ii) such person shall not be so released if such offence is a cognizable offence and he had been previously convicted of an offence punishable with death, imprisonment for life or imprisonment for seven years or more, or he had been previously convicted on two or more occasions of a non-bailable and cognizable offence:

Provided that the court may direct that a person referred to in clause (i) or clause (ii) be released on bail if such person is under the age of sixteen years or is a woman or is sick or infirm:

Provided further that the court may also direct that a person referred to in clause (ii) be released on bail if it is satisfied that it is just and proper so to do for any other special reason:

Provided also that the mere fact that an accused person may be required for being identified by witnesses during investigation shall not be sufficient ground for refusing to grant bail if he is otherwise entitled to be released on bail and gives an undertaking that he shall comply with such directions as may be given by the court.

(2) If it appears to such officer or court at any stage of the investigation, inquiry or trial, as the case may be, that there are not reasonable grounds for believing that the accused has committed a non-bailable offence, but that there are sufficient grounds for further inquiry into his guilt, the accused shall, subject to the provisions of section 446A and pending such inquiry, be released on bail, or at the discretion of such officer or Court, on the execution by him of a bond without sureties for his appearance as hereinafter provided.

(3) When a person accused or suspected of the commission of an offence punishable with imprisonment which may extend to

seven years or more or of an offence under Chapter VI, Chapter XVI or Chapter XVII of the Indian Penal Code (45 of 1860) or abetment of, or conspiracy or attempt to commit, any such offence, is released on bail under sub-section (1), the court may impose any condition which the Court considers necessary –

(a) in order to ensure that such person shall attend in accordance with the condition of the bond executed under this Chapter, or

(b) in order to ensure that such person shall not commit an offence similar to the offence of which he is accused or of the commission of which he is suspected, or

(c) otherwise in the interests of justice

(4) An officer or a court releasing any person on bail under subsection (1) or subsection (2), shall record in writing his or its reasons or special reasons for so doing.

(5) Any court which has released a person on bail under sub-section (1) or subsection (2), may, if it considers it necessary so to do, direct that such person be arrested and commit him to custody.

(6) If, in any case triable by a Magistrate, the trial of a person, accused of any non-bailable offence is not concluded within a period of sixty days from the first day fixed for taking evidence in the case, such person shall, if he is in custody during the whole of the said period, be released on bail to the satisfaction of the Magistrate, unless for reasons to be recorded in writing, the Magistrate otherwise directs.

(7) If, at any time after the conclusion of the trial of a person accused of a non-bailable offence and before judgment is delivered, the court is of opinion that there are reasonable grounds for believing that the accused is not guilty of any such offence, it shall release the accused, if he is in custody, on the execution by him of a bond without sureties for his appearance to hear judgment delivered.

BIBLIOGRAPHY

1. Corbin, A., 1990,. *Women for Hire :Prostitution and Sexuality in France after 1850*. Harvard University Press, Cambridge.
2. Levy, Jay A., 1990. *Changing Concepts of HIV Infection : Challenges for the 1990s.*
3. Joardar, Biswanath, 1984, *Prostitution in Historical and Modern Perspectives*, Inter-India Publications, New Delhi.
4. Berer Marge and Ray Sunanda, (1993). *Women and HIV/ AIDS*, In International Resource Book.
5. O'Neill, Maggie. 'Prostitute Women Now,' In Scambler, Graham and Annette Scambler (Eds). *Rethinking Prostitution : Purchasing Sex in the 1990s*, Routledge, London.
6. Punekar, S.D. and Rao Kamala, 1967. *A Study of Prostitution in Bombay*, Lalwarie Publishing House, Mumbai.
7. Brown Phyllida, *How Does HIV Cause AIDS.*
8. Rozario, Sr. M. Rita, 1988 *Trafficking in Women and Children in India: Sexual Exploitation and Sale*, Uppal Publishing House, Mumbai.
9. Scambler, Graham and Scambler, Annette (Eds). 1997. *Rethinking Prostitution: Purchasing Sex in the 1990s*, Routledge, London.
10. Thukral, Enakshi Ganguly, "Girl-Child and Children: The Plight of India's Children," *The Times of India*, 24th April 1996.
11. Thomas, E.J. and Jose Elsamma, 1991. Prostitution — A Kerala Profile, *Loyola Journal of Social Sciences*, Vol. V., No. 1, pp. 48-64.
12. Henian Y, et. al. 1990, *Prevalence of HIV in Cervico-vaginal Secretion of Women Seropositive for HIV*".
13. World Health Organisation, Press Release. "*AIDS: Over a Million New Infections in 8 Months*, Geneva, 12th Feb. 1992.
14. Shanker, Uday, *Exceptional Children*, Published by S.K. Ghai, Mg. Director, Sterling Publishers (P) Ltd., AB/9, Safdarjang Enclave, New Delhi - 110016.
15. Banerjee, Gauri Rani, *Papers on Social Work – An Indian*

Perspective, Published by Tata Institute of Social Sciences, Mumbai-88.

16. Kashappagoudar, N.B., 1988. Prostitution and the Law, *Social Welfare,* Vol. XXXV, No. 4, July 1988.
17. Joint Women's Programme Bangalore, 1988, *Banhi-Devadasi System in North Karnataka.*
18. Pawar, M.S. 1988. Trafficking in Women-Can Legislation Stop the Evil? *Social Welfare,* Vol. XXXV, No. 4, July 1998.
19. Rozaio, Sr. M. Rita, assisted by Javed Rasool and Pradeep Kesari, 1988. *Trafficking in Women and Children in India: A Joint Women's Programme Publication,* Published by Uppal Publishing House, 3, Ansari Road, Daryaganj, New Delhi - 110002.
20. Mishra, Sashi, 1989. An Action Plan for Street Children, *Social Welfare Journal,* Vol. XXXVI, No. 6, Sept., 1989.
21. Bhaskaran, A report on National Workshop on Prostitutes and their Children, *Social Welfare Journal,* Vol. XXXVII, July 1990.
22. Das, Rajita and Chopra, Romila, 1990,. Prostitution-How to Deal with it? *Social Welfare Journal;* Vol. XXXVI; No. 3, June 1990.
23. Department of Women and Child Development Government of India and UNICEF India, Co-ordinated by Nirmala Niketan College of Social Work, Mumbai, 1996; Draft Declaration and Agenda for action—Regional Workshop on Sexual Exploitation and Trafficking of Children.
24. Jogin Shankar, 1996. Profile of Karnataka—A State's Paper Presented at Regional Workshop on Sexual Exploitation and Trafficking of Children.
25. Khan, Ali, Mumtaz, 1996. Street Girls and Immoral Traffic in India - Under the auspices of Centre for Research and Development of Dalits, Bangalore - 560 032 (India), Published by-Uppal Publishing House, 3 Ansari Road, Daryaganj, New Delhi - 110002.
26. Mander, Harsh and Rao, Vidya, 1996. An Agenda for Caring Interventions for Marginalised Groups, General Editor: Dr. V.K. Agnihotri, Funded by Ministry of Welfare and Department of Women and Child Welfare Ministry of Human Resource Development (Government of India)

published by Voluntary Health Association of India, Tong Swasthya Bhavan, 40, Institutional Area, near Qutab Hotel, New Delhi.

27. National Institute of Public Cooperation and Child Development, 1996. Statistics on Children in India, Pocket Book, Published by: National Institute of Public Cooperation and Child Development, 5, Siri Institutional Area, Hauz Khas, New Delhi - 110016.
28. Nayak Nina, P. (1996). The World's Dirtiest Business: What can be done to Stop the Child Sex Trade, A paper presented at NGO Forum on Child Abuse held at Bangalore organised by Madhyam, Bangalore.
29. Rao, Amla Rama, (1990). The Health Status of the Prostitutes and their Children, *Social Welfare Journal,* Vol. - XXXVII, No. 3, June 1990.
30. Singh, Y.N., (1990). Health Needs of Prostitutes, *Social Welfare Journal,* Vol. XXXVII, No. 4, July, 1990.
31. UNESCO (1991); Adolescence Education—Physical and Psychological Aspect Module One & Two; Published by UNESCO Principal Regional Office for Asia and the Pacific, P.O. Box 967, Prakanorg Post Office, Bangkok - 10110, Thailand.
32. D'Cunha, Jean (1992). Prostitution Laws-Ideological Dimensions and Enforcement Practices, *Economic and Political Weekly,* Vol. XXXVII, No. 17, April 25, 1992.
33. Department of Women and Child Development, Government of India (1994). Child Prostitution—In the Twilight? A Status and Action Report of the Central Advisory Committee on Child Prostitution; Published by Department of Women and Child Development, Ministry of Human Resource Development, Government of India.
34. Verma, Paripumand 1994; Sex offences in India and Abroad, B.R. Publishing Corporation, Delhi - 110052.
35. YMCA, ECPAT and UNICEF , 1995. *Child Prostitution: The Ultimate Abuse,* Report on the National Consultation on Child Prostitution held on 18-20 Nov., 1995, New Delhi.
36. Pandey, Divya, 1996; Commercial Sex Workers in India; Newsletter, Research Centre for Women's Studies, Published by S.N.D.T. Women's University, Sir Vithaldas Vidyavihar, Juhu Road, Mumbai-49.

37. Joshi, Madhu D. (ed) 1997. Women and Children in Prostitution. Human Rights Perspectives (Report of National Workshop); A Joint Women's Programme Publication. Uppal Publishing House, New Delhi-2.
38. Ghosh, S.K, 1997. *The World of Prostitutes,* Vols. I & II; A.P.H., Publishing Corporation; 5 Ansari Road, Daryaganj, New Delhi - 110002.
39. Women's Study Development Centre, University of Delhi, 1992: They too are Children, A report on the Rehabilitation of Children of Prostitutes, Sponsored by Dept. of Welfare, Govt. of India, Delhi.
40. UNICEF, 1994, March, The Child & The Law—India Country Office.
41. JWP, 1988. Bamhi, Prostitution with Religious Sanction; The Devadasi Problem, Venkatasani/Jogini, and Basavi Cult—JWP Publication.
42. 1996, Checking Child Prostitution, *The Hindu,* May 3, 1996.
43. Gupta, R, 1996. Children for Sale, *Asia Week,* March 1, 1996, Mumbai.
44. Mittal, L.N, 1996, Feb. Child Prostitution and Sex Tourism, *Social Welfare,* Vol. 42, No. 11. pp. 26-27.
45. UBINIG, Bangladesh, 1995. Pamphlet on Trafficking in Women and Children, The Case of Bangladesh, Narigrantha Prabartana, (The Feminist Bookstore), 2/8, Sir Syed Road, Mohammadpur, Dhaka - 1207, Bangladesh.
46. Rohde, J.E. Elial, 1996, India's Shame : The Prostitution of Children, paper presented at National Meeting on Prostitution by National Commission for Women, ICCR, Azad Bhawan, Delhi.
47. Prayas, 1994, A Study of Initiatives in the Rescue and Rehabilitation, or Amelioration of the Situation of Women and Girls in Prostitution in India, Tata Institute of Social Sciences, Sponsored by National Commission for Women, New Delhi.
48. Govt. of India, 1995, Crime in India, National Crime Records Bureau, Ministry of Home Affairs, Standardization in Police.
49. Bedi, M.S., 1992. *Protection of Women in Moral Danger,* Himanshu Publications, Udaipur.
50. Shankar, Jogan, 1994. *Devadasi Cult; A Sociological Analysis,*

Ashish Publishing House, 8/81, Punjabi Bagh, New Delhi - 110026.

51. State Commission for Women, 1996, Exploiting Children for Commercial Sex—A rapid appraisal in the State of Orissa, State Commission for Women, Orissa.
52. Zilla Panchayat, Karnataka State Women's Development Corporation and Myrada, 1991, Devadasi Rehabilitation Project, Belgaum, Project Headquarters, near Syndicate Bank, Doopdal Road, Ghataprabha - 591306, Dist Belgaum, Karnataka, India.
53. Dept. of Women and Child Development, 1994, National Workshop on Prostitutes and their Children, Ministry of Human Welfare, Govt. of India.
54. Selvaraj, S.J., 1996. Is Prostitution a Sin?, *Women's Link*, July-Sept., pp. 41-43.
55. UMED, 1996, Sexual Abuse and the Growth of Paedophilia: A Regional Profile of Goa, presented at UNICEF / Dept. of Women and Child Development Workshop, 29-30th May 1996, Goa.
56. Baria, Farah, 1996, "Child Abuse: Sexual Outrage on the Beach", *India Today*, March 31.
57. Dias, Fiona, 1993, Jan., "*Child Abuse: A Growing Concern;* VHAI, Delhi.
58. Suresh, K.T. and Noronha, Rico, 1991. Nov., Situating the Role of Tourism in Child Prostitution, paper presented at 3rd SAARC Conference on the Rights of the Child, Calcutta.
59. Indian Council of Social Welfare, AP and College of Social Work, Hyderabad, 1991. A Study of Gender Victims in the Twin Cities of Hyderabad and Secunderabad, a research project sponsored by ICSW - A.P., Red Hills, Hyderabad - 500004.
60. INSAF, 1996. Child Prostitution in Western India, report of workshop, with support from UNICEF, Delhi, *Insaf*, Goa.
61. Rakesh, K.M., 1997. Along the Coast, the 'Ghosts' of Perversity, *The Sunday Statesman*, Impressions, Sunday, Jan. 19, 1997.
62. Saxena, Rashmi, 1996, The Young and the Damned, cover story on Child Prostitutes, *The Week*, Aug. 4, 1996, pp. 40-42.

63. Ganguli, T. and Abraham, M., 1997. Body Shoppers, *The Week,* Feb. 16, 1997.
64. Central Social Welfare Board, 1993. Prostitution in Metropolitan Cities of India, CSWB, Samaj Kalyan Bhawan, B-12, Tara Crescent, Institutional Area, South of IIT, New Delhi - 110016.
65. National Council of Churches in India, Urban Rural Mission, 1997, Report of the Meeting on Campaign of Child Prostitution in India, Panaji, Goa.
66. Havelock, Ellis, 1936. Psychology of Sex, New York, Random House, Vol. II.
67. Kinsey, Alfred C., 1948. Sexual Behaviour in Human Male, London : W.B. Saunders Company.
68. Basu, N.K. and Sinha, W.S.N., 1929, History of Prostitution in India, Bengal Social Hygiene Association, Calcutta.
69. Kapur, Promilla, 1978. The Life and World of Call Girls in India, Vikas Publishing House Pvt. Ltd, New Delhi.
70. 1991, Sept., Conclusions of the General Rapporteur, Council of Europe : Seminar on Action against Traffic in Women and Forced Prostitution as Violations of Human Rights and Human Dignity.
71. Joint Action Council for Women, 1996, Feb., Proceedings of Workshop, Chennai.
72. Chatterjee, A . and Sehgal, K., 1994. HIV/AIDS Awareness and Courts, 19 NGOs experiences in Delhi, Maharashtra, and Tamil Nadu, Ford Foundation, New Delhi.
73. Atma Pariksha, 1993, Draft Report of Consultation with Community based HIV Prevention and Care Projects, UNDP, HIV and Development.
74. Bhaiya, Abha and Kapur, Ratna, 1994. March, Report of the National Workshop on Women, STDs, HIV and AIDS, Jagori, New Delhi.
75. 1996 April, Report; West Bengal State Conference; Mahila Samanvaya Committee, Calcutta.
76. Joint Women's Programme, 1996. Dec., Seminar on Women in Prostitution—A Human Rights Perspective, JWP, New Delhi.
77. Davis, Kingsley, 1937. "The Sociology of Prostitution, *American Sociological Review*, Vol. II, No. 5.
78. Davis, Kingsley, 1966. "Sexual Behaviour" Contemporary

Social Problems (ed.) by Merton and Nisbet, II, edi, New York : Hari Court, Brace and World, Inc.

79. D'Cunha, Jean, 1991. *The Legalisation of Prostitution: A Sociological Inquiry into Laws Relating to Prostitution in India and the West,* Wordmakers, Bangalore.
80. Hofmann, Cecelia, 1997. Is it a Human Right to Prostitute? Women in Action, No. 2, pp. 28-36.
81. Solanki, Gopika and Gangoli, G., 1996, The Official Discourse Around PITA, EPW, Vol. XXXI, No. 51.
82. Ministry of Welfare, 1987. Prostitution and Immoral Traffic Encyclopaedia of Social Work in India, Vol. II, pp. 346-354.
83. Acknowledgement: Human Rights on Duty, Mary O'Rawe & Dr. Linda Moore.
84. Acknowledgment: The Human Right Watch Global Report on Women's Human Rights.

Index